WALKING by FAITH

Liturgy and Ritual Book

Robert W. Piercy, Jr.
and
David Haas

Other resources in the series:
Compact Disc and Cassette • CD/CS-412
Full Score • G-4831FS
Student Melody Book • G-4831P

GIA Publications, Inc.

For permission to reprint copyrighted material, grateful acknowledgment is made to the following sources:

International Committee on English in the Liturgy, Inc. (ICEL): Excerpts from the English translation of *Lectionary for Mass* ©1969, 1981 by ICEL. From the English translation of *The Roman Missal* © 1973 by ICEL. From the English translation of *Eucharistic Prayers for Masses with Children* © 1975 by ICEL. From the English translation of *Book of Blessings* © 1988 by ICEL. From the English translations of *Pastoral Care of the Sick: Rites of Anointing and Viaticum* © 1982 by ICEL. From the English translation of *Rite of Confirmation,* Second Edition © 1975 by ICEL. All rights reserved.

American Bible Society: All Scripture verses from *THE HOLY BIBLE: Contemporary English Version,* © 1995, American Bible Society. Used by permission.

Grade 2, Unit 3 Opening Prayer: Adapted from "Blessing of an Advent Wreath" from *Catholic Household Blessings and Prayers,* Copyright © 1988, United States Catholic Conference, Inc., Washington, D.C. Used with permission. All rights reserved.

Grade 3, Unit 4 Opening Prayer: Adapted from *Catholic Household Blessings and Prayers,* Copyright © 1988, United States Catholic Conference, Inc. Used with permission. All rights reserved.

Grade 5, Unit 1 Opening Prayer: Excerpt from the *Book of Common Prayer,* copyright © Church Pension Fund

Cover illustrations by Linda Messier, Lori Lohstoeter, Bill James, Linda Montgomery, Kathy Petrauskas, and Francis Livingston.

Book design and layout by Robert M. Sacha

Printed in the United States of America

ISBN 0-15-950532-1

10 9 8 7 6 5 4 3 2 1

WALKING BY FAITH
TABLE OF CONTENTS

Grade Three—The Church

Grade Four—Christian Morality

Grade Five—The Sacraments

Grade Six—Salvation History

Introduction

LITURGY AND MUSIC IN CATECHESIS

Catechesis and liturgy go hand in hand. Although the catechist may be called to form young people in the celebration of the liturgy, the liturgy itself has the power to do the forming. This is done by celebrating liturgy well and allowing children to grow into the experience of ritual. Look at it through the lens of going to school. No one taught us "how" to go to school, we simply learned from experience. In the experience someone may show us proper manners or behavior, proper language or gestures, but the overall experience was learned by "doing." Such is the way with liturgy. Too often, we who are catechists feel we need to "teach" children everything they need to know before they ever attend a liturgical celebration. This does not have to happen. Instead, let us try to celebrate liturgies with dignity, awe, and wonder. Through these celebrations children will come to know the power of liturgy in their prayer life and in their very existence.

Walking by Faith gives catechists such an opportunity. BROWN-ROA should be applauded for wanting to gather many components into their curriculum. Using all of our senses, the *Walking by Faith* journey calls us to celebrate what we believe as Catholics, and it enables us to ritualize these experiences. When developing these services, special attention was given to age-appropriate texts and music that was appropriate for liturgy–not only in the catechetical setting but also in the parish liturgy. This book is intended for directors and coordinators of religious education programs and principals, grade level catechists and teachers, and their assistants. This book is also very important for presiders, liturgists, and musicians of the parish. It has the following companion pieces:

Walking by Faith CD and cassette with original music by David Haas
Walking by Faith Full Score with reproducible melody boxes
Walking by Faith Student Melody Book with music for refrains and texts of verses

All of these are available from GIA Publications, Inc. (1-800-GIA-1358), or BROWN-ROA (1-800-922-7696).

These services are built around the *Walking by Faith* curriculum concepts for grades K through 6: Creation, God, Jesus Christ, The Church, Christian Morality, The Sacraments, and Salvation History. For each grade level there are seven prayer services, each celebrating one of the above mentioned ideas. There are also five school- or parish-wide celebrations. These celebrations are for the Beginning of the Catechetical Year, Advent, Lent, a Reconciliation Service, and End of the Catechetical Year. Although your parish or school may not be using the full *Walking by Faith* program, these rituals will still be appropriate for any religious education program because GIA and BROWN-ROA are sensitive and knowledgeable on the spiritual development of children.

SCHOOL- OR PARISH-WIDE CELEBRATIONS

Let's look at the school- or parish-wide celebrations first. Ideally these would be celebrated with everyone in the program, including members of the parish community not directly involved in catechesis. When you approach this liturgy you will notice that it takes on the substance of a Eucharistic celebration. That is the ideal setting for these celebrations (excluding the Reconciliation service). Understanding that not all programs have the luxury of being able to celebrate Eucharist with an ordained priest, other options are given. Please note that when a non-ordained presider is celebrating, the greeting at the beginning of the liturgy is different. For further information on this, consult *Sunday Celebrations in the Absence of a Priest* (USCC or Catholic Book Publishing) and *Catholic Household Blessings and Prayers* (USCC, Catholic Book Publishing, or Liturgical Press).

Whatever is celebrated is still considered liturgy, despite the differences between a Eucharistic liturgy and a non-Eucharistic liturgy. Careful discussion with the parish catechetical and liturgy team needs to be done. Discuss which version is appropriate in your situation and who should preside when a non-ordained minister is necessary. When celebrating these liturgies as non-Eucharistic ones, take note of the form to follow: After the reflection is given, which may be given by a lay minister (see *Directory for Masses with Children,* par. 24), there should be some silence before moving into the next section. Sometimes a canticle is then sung or the movement is right into the general intercessions, followed by the Lord's Prayer and Concluding Rite.

If you are doing a Eucharistic celebration, use the *Sacramentary* after the homily-Scripture reflection and return to the text in this book for the Concluding Rite.

It is assumed that the Scripture proclaimed will be from the *Lectionary for Masses with Children* promulgated for use by the National Conference of Catholic Bishops of the United States on November 28, 1993. The translation for this Scripture is from the *Contemporary English Version* by the American Bible Society in New York City. For further information on this lectionary, consult *A Guide to the Lectionary for Masses with Children* (Liturgy Training Publications, 1-800-933-1800). For information on the CEV translation, contact the American Bible Society, (1-800-32-BIBLE).

Each school- or parish-wide celebration is followed by the process called *mystagogy*. This is a time of allowing all who participated to reflect on their experience. For years this has been done with catechumens and candidates after the Easter Vigil. The directions are quite specific and will enhance other catechetical moments. It is suggested that you try a mystagogy as a group of catechists first to see how it is done. The director of your catechumenate program may have other suggestions for celebrating mystagogy.

For more information on specifics of celebrating liturgies, consult *When Children Gather: 20 Eucharistic Liturgies for the School Year* (GIA 1-800-GIA-1358). Excellent principles and ideas for celebrating liturgies throughout the year are given in this book.

GRADE SPECIFIC LITURGIES

The grade specific liturgies correspond with the first three chapters of every grade unit–K through 6. There are seven units per grade, thus a total of 49 prayer services. Although these could be celebrated as Eucharistic liturgies (you may need to make some modifications), the original intent was to have the catechist or teacher preside at these services. If your program has more than one section of a grade level (let's say three sections of students in grade three), you may want to gather all the grade-level students together to celebrate this service. Remember–these liturgies are written in such a way that any number of students can take part in the prayer. Do not hesitate in celebrating these services. Let's walk through these services step by step.

Time and Place of Service

Before you begin your unit, look at the prayer service and decide when it would best fit into the material that is covered. The place for this service should be any place that is designated as your catechetical prayer space. If you can't leave your room, set up a corner for prayer. Have a table with a CEV Bible, a symbol (cross, water, plant, candle, or all of these things), and a chair for the presider. If possible, find another place you may want to have these celebrations. Is there a place outside? Maybe a place in the church would be available, or perhaps you can at least move to another room. Anywhere that suggests that the space is holy and that the assembly is to give praise and glory to God is appropriate. Maybe the parish environment and art committee can offer suggestions. Be creative!

Getting Started

These are simple notes that will help you prepare yourself as the lay presider. Remember that at the moment of prayer, you are NO LONGER a catechist or teacher but a presider of the community's prayer. It may be helpful to ask your DRE or principal to review this role with you and the other catechists or teachers. In this section you are also alerted to anything specific you will need for a ritual action. Take a little time before your class to prepare these things so as not to go on a frantic scavenger hunt prior to or worse yet, during prayer.

Music Suggestions

The music for these services all come from the recording *Walking by Faith* by David Haas and Robert Piercy. The music is integral to the prayer. Use the CD or cassette as a tool for learning the music. Trust yourself and the students to sing the songs *a cappella*, if necessary. However, don't feel you have to use these songs. They are suggestions. Included on p. 147 is a list of other musical suggestions that would work in these prayer services. Also look at what the students are singing at the Sunday liturgy. Perhaps one of those songs would be more appro-priate. Full scores of the music are available, as are student melody books. Before copying anything, check on copyright permissions with your DRE, principal, or liturgist.

Introductory Rites

Although technically not Eucharistic celebrations, these services were designed to form children in the prayers and gestures that would be celebrated during a Eucharist. Use ritual language and NOT your own words. "The Lord be with you. Hi! How are you today?" would not be appropriate. Children will grow in their awe and wonder of the liturgy if you stick to the script. On the other hand, the Opening Comment could be in your own words. This is a time when you set the mood for what you are about to do. Use images that would be appropriate for your students.

The Opening Prayer was usually adapted from a prayer on the *We Celebrate* pages of the *Walking by Faith* textbooks. There is a proper gesture to be used here. It is called the "orans" gesture, and means that the arms and hands are extended in an open fashion. This is not to be confused with the gesture for "The Lord be with you." That gesture is called an invitatory gesture. For "The Lord be with you" see diagram A. For the orans gesture used in the Opening Prayer, see diagram B.

Diagram A

Invitatory gesture

Diagram B

Orans gesture

Scripture Reading

The Scripture was taken from a suggested Scripture for the chapters covered in this service. Additional verses may have been added.
Please note: Even though the Scripture was provided here, this was simply for presider preparation. When you are proclaiming Scripture in the service, it is of extreme importance that you actually read from the Bible. A lectionary would not be as helpful here as would a worthy-looking Bible. Again, use a *Contemporary English Version* translation (American Bible Society). This translation is wonderful for liturgies with children in grade levels K through 6. The ritual action of reverencing the Bible and picking it up to read is very important. Mark the reading prior to the service.

The minister for this reading could be a child if he or she is prepared and can proclaim for all to hear. Perhaps an aide, or another catechist or teacher, or even a parish lector can help with these services. When children see lectors from their "Sunday celebration," they may be inspired to be lectors one day.

The reflection questions provided are NOT questions to ask the students. Rather, they are questions to ask yourself to help you organize your thoughts. A Scripture reflection should communicate:

• What happened in the Scripture passage

- What the Scripture passage means to you
- How it challenges you in your life

The reflection should be short. Remember, here you are not a catechist or teacher but a co-journeyer in the children's spiritual journey. You may ask the children questions, but don't make them test questions on the Scripture. They should be questions on what the passage means to the children. Further study on preparing a reflection can be found in the document *Fulfilled in Your Hearing* (United States Catholic Conference, 1982).

Ritual Action

When a ritual action takes place, it needs to be thought through. How can this ritual be done without losing the sacredness of what you are doing? Many of the ritual actions are taken from actions that are done in parish liturgies. You may wish to discuss these with the people who prepare the liturgies in your parish. How are these actions–venerating a cross, washing of feet, laying on of hands–done in your setting? Please do not ignore these rituals. Often it your chance to pray quietly with each child. Silence, even if for a moment, can be highly effective.

The Lord's Prayer

The text alluded to here is the traditional/liturgical form for this prayer. Since these liturgies form children in the ways of the Church, the proper posture for this prayer would be the one used by your community–holding hands, orans position, or hands held reverently in front of your body.

Concluding Rite

You are encouraged to sing the final blessing. The final song on the CD or cassette is "Final Blessing," a wonderful setting done by David Haas based on the melody of "Adoro Te Devote." If you cannot sing this melody, then speak the text that is given. Always end your celebration with the dismissal form, i.e., "Our celebration has ended . . . " and a concluding song.

Although there are many things to consider, once you have done one service, the others will fall into place. These services are built on the concept that repetition of style is good. Don't keep changing how you do the services. What changes is who you are and who the students are. Your life and their lives change day to day. Celebrate this in the constancy of prayer. Never feel that you are alone when presiding. You are the conduit for the child's prayer. Consult with your grade level coordinator, DRE, principal, and other presiders of the parish community. Have them share with you their experiences and ideas that they may have that would allow you to enter into a spirit of holiness and prayer. Allow the spirit of Christ's love to work through you.

Peace in your ministry.

Liturgy for the Beginning of the Catechetical Year

Getting Started

As you look over this liturgy, be sure that the children know their responses. Also be sure that the catechists know to come forward for the blessing after the Sign of Peace. You may want to go over the reading with the students prior to the liturgy. Anyone ministering at this liturgy should have rehearsed their role.

INTRODUCTORY RITES

Opening Song
"Walking by Faith," CD/CS–#1, music book–#1

Greeting
Presider: In the name of the Father, and of the Son, and of the Holy Spirit.
All: **Amen!**

Presider: The Lord be with you.
All: **And also with you.**

Or if the presider is a lay minister:

Presider: Let us praise the God of wisdom, knowledge, and grace.
Blessed be God for ever.
All: **Blessed be God for ever.**

Opening Comments
Presider: As we gather to celebrate the beginning of our journey of walking by faith, we realize that we come from different experiences. These experiences will help make our journey this year different and new. Let us begin this journey by presenting ourselves to God.

Opening Prayer
Presider: Let us pray. *(orans gesture)*
God of new beginnings,
you call us to walk with you this year and to be strong in our faith.
May we walk with one another in peace and love,
being open to your words,
and willing to learn all that is put before us.
We praise you as the God who lives and reigns for ever and ever. Amen.

LITURGY OF THE WORD

First Reading
Colossians 2:6–7, *Lectionary for Masses with Children,* #216

Responsorial Psalm
"God's People" (Psalm 100), CD/CS–#2, mb–#2
Silence

SCHOOL- OR PARISH-WIDE LITURGIES: BEGINNING OF YEAR

Gospel Acclamation

"Alleluia/Gospel Acclamation," *(sing verse 1)*, CD/CS–#5, mb–#5

Gospel

John 1:35–40, *Lectionary for Masses with Children, #60*

Homily (Scripture Reflection)

When preparing your homily or reflection, consider these questions:
1. *How do you view Jesus as a teacher?*
2. *Who has formed you in your religious education?*
3. *Why do you follow Jesus?*
4. *What challenges you in this new year of catechesis?*

Gospel Canticle *(use only in non-Eucharistic celebrations)*
"Blest Are You, O God" (Canticle of Zachary), CD/CS–#7, mb–#7

GENERAL INTERCESSIONS

These are the General Intercessions found in the music collection.

Presider: Let us present our needs to the Lord.

Cantor: *(intones or reads)*
For all who belong to the Catholic Church and all who teach us **about** God. *Cantor sings:* Let us pray to the Lord.

All: *Sung response or:* **Lord, hear our prayer.**

Cantor: For our country and our need to always work for peace.
Cantor sings: Let us pray to the Lord.

For those who are without food or without a home.
Cantor sings: Let us pray to the Lord.

For all those who walk by faith, celebrating God's love in **all the world.**
Cantor sings: Let us pray to the Lord.

For all who are sick and await God's loving touch.
Cantor sings: Let us pray to the Lord.

For those who have died, and who now live for ever with **God.**
Cantor sings: Let us pray to the Lord.

Presider: God of hopes and dreams,
your Spirit calls us to be people of peace.
May we walk by faith, confident that you are always **with us.**
We praise you with Christ Jesus, for ever and ever. Amen!

If you are doing a Eucharistic liturgy, proceed to Liturgy of the Eucharist in the Sacramentary and return to this prayer service for the final blessing. If you are not doing a Eucharistic celebration, continue here.

LORD'S PRAYER

Presider: Let us now join in the words Christ himself has given us.

All: **Our Father . . . for the kingdom, the power, and the glory are yours, now and for ever. Amen.**

Sign of Peace

Presider: Lord Jesus Christ, you said to your apostles: I leave you peace, my peace I give you. Look not on our sins, but on the faith of your Church, and grant us the peace and unity of your kingdom where you live for ever and ever.

All: **Amen.**

Presider: Let us offer each other the sign of peace.

CONCLUDING RITE

Blessing
"Final Blessing," CD/CS–#19, mb–#25

Blessing for Catechists
Use the following instead of the blessing prayer found in "Final Blessing."

Presider: I invite the catechists to come forward for a blessing.

May God bless the work you do as you share the word of God
with your children this year.
May Christ show you ways of peace and understanding.
May the Holy Spirit inspire your hearts and your minds.
And may God bless you, the Father, and the Son, ✠ and the Holy Spirit.
Amen.
Sing "Final Blessing" again.

Dismissal

Presider: Let us go forth, walking by faith, to love and serve our God.
All: **Thanks be to God.**

Closing Song
"Deep Down I Know," CD/CS–#10, mb–#12 or "Walking by Faith," CD/CS–#1, mb–#1

MYSTAGOGY

Mystagogy is the time spent after a service during which the students reflect on their experience. Invite the students to use all their senses to concentrate on the total experience of the service—what they saw, heard, gestured, participated in, sung, and so on. Use the following process:

1 *First have the children close their eyes and remember what happened. You may want to talk through the service yourself and have the children simply remember.*

2. Have the children tell you what they remember. Use this as a time for brainstorming. Can they reconstruct the service for you and tell you what was important to them?

3. Ask them what the liturgy meant to them. Was there something that happened that connected with their own life?

4. Ask them to describe how they are feeling or how they felt during the celebration. It is important to go for feeling words—sad, happy, awestruck, confused, and so on. These will facilitate your ability to further the discussion. Ask if any others felt this way.

5. Finally, have them ask any question they may have. Understand that you don't have to have all the answers but tell them you will find out the answer, or together you might do some research.

6. Close with a prayer from the service and ask the children to remember silently, in their hearts, something very special about this service and how this will affect their relationship with God.

Liturgy During the Season of Advent

Getting Started

This celebration should happen sometime during Unit Three. Classes should prepare for this liturgy by reviewing the readings. If possible, take a trip to the church and look at the Advent wreath. Talk about different types of Advent wreaths and about your own understanding of this symbol.

Take a special look at the music for this service. David Haas has done a wonderful weaving of song and prayer in the opening rites. The responsorial psalm for this liturgy (Psalm 25) is based upon the traditional Advent melody of "O Come, O Come, Emmanuel." The canticle used ("Holy Is Your Name") is the Canticle of Mary. This canticle is also used as the gospel canticle for Evening Prayer.

Consider gathering at the Advent wreath in your space, wherever it may be. The Introductory Rite takes on special beauty if you gather in the dark. You could also consider using older students as candle bearers. After the Advent wreath candles have been lit, light the candles held by the candle bearers and do a procession of light. You may want to enhance the procession with incense. Even if the wreath is in the sanctuary, gather there and then process to your pews.

INTRODUCTORY RITES

Opening Song

"Make Ready the Way" from Advent Gathering, CD/CS–#3, mb–#3
Sing as you gather near the Advent wreath. The following is spoken over Musical Interlude I.

Greeting

Presider: In the name of the Father, and of the Son, and of the Holy Spirit.
All: **Amen!**

Presider: The Lord be with you.
All: **And also with you.**

Or if the presider is a lay minister:

Presider: Light and peace in Jesus Christ, our Lord.
All: **Thanks be to God.**

Blessing of Advent Wreath

Presider: We praise you, God of new beginnings.
We welcome this Season of Advent.
We praise you for the gift of this Advent wreath.
May the candles and evergreens on this wreath
light our way this season.
We praise you for giving us Jesus, the Light of the World!

"Come, O Lord" follows. During the song, the presider lights the Advent wreath candles and then the processional candles. Then all process to their places in church. Over Musical Interlude II, the following is prayed:

Opening Prayer

Presider: Let us pray. *(orans gesture)*
O God, you created the entire universe and everything in it.
You show love to everyone.
You overlook our wrongdoing.
We, your children, turn to you.
As we walk in faith this season, we are invited to explore,
reflect, and celebrate your gift to humankind.
May we be light to a darkened world,
and may we share faith with each other,
as we proclaim that you are God, for ever and ever. Amen.

Sing refrain of "Come, O Lord."

Presider: Let us be seated. *(extinguish candles)*

LITURGY OF THE WORD

First Reading
Isaiah 40:25–26, 29–31, *Lectionary for Masses with Children*, #174

Responsorial Psalm
"To You, O Lord" (Psalm 25), CD/CS–#6, mb–#6
Silence

Gospel Acclamation
"Alleluia/Gospel Acclamation," CD/CS–#5, mb–#5 *(sing verse 3)*

Gospel
Luke 1:46–56, *Lectionary for Masses with Children*, #175

Homily (Scripture Reflection)
While preparing your homily or reflection, consider these questions:
1. *What in creation excites you the most? What is it about this "thing" that makes you celebrate?*
2. *What are you waiting for in your life this Advent Season, and what are your feelings about this waiting?*

If you are doing a Eucharistic liturgy, proceed to Liturgy of the Eucharist in the Sacramentary and return to this prayer service for the final blessing. If you are not doing a Eucharistic celebration, continue here.

Presider: Continuing our celebration, let us stand and sing the words of our Blessed Mother.

Gospel Canticle
"Holy Is Your Name" (Canticle of Mary), CD/CS–#4, mb–#4

GENERAL
INTERCESSIONS

For the response, sing the refrain of "Come, O Lord," from "Advent Gathering," CD/CS–#3, mb–#3.

Presider: In the glow of this Advent light, let us come before God with the needs of our hearts.

Cantor: *(intones or reads)*
For our Church and all who help see the peace of Christ.
Let us pray to the Lord. *All sing: "Come, O Lord . . ."*

For the world and all who seek peace during this season.
Let us pray to the Lord. *All sing: "Come, O Lord . . ."*

For those who are without the shelter of warmth this season.
Let us pray to the Lord. *All sing: "Come, O Lord . . ."*

Include local intercessions here.

For those who are ill and seek the healing touch of Christ.
Let us pray to the Lord. *All sing: "Come, O Lord . . ."*

For those who have died and now live in the eternal light of God.
Let us pray to the Lord. *All sing: "Come, O Lord . . ."*

LORD'S PRAYER
Presider: Let us join in the words that Christ himself has given us.

All: **Our Father . . . for the kingdom, the power, and glory are yours, now and for ever. Amen.**

CONCLUDING RITE
Presider:

Closing Prayer
Let us pray.
God of light,
be a source of strength to us in this Advent Season.
May our time together be productive and filled with the holiness of your awe and wonder.
May we praise you as the God who lives and reigns for ever and ever.
Amen.

Blessing
"Final Blessing," CD/CS–#19, mb–#25, or:

Solemn Blessing

Presider: Let us bow our heads and ask for God's blessing.

May Christ's coming bring us light and bless our journey.

All: **Amen!**

Presider: May God make us joyful in hope and untiring in love
as we walk by faith.

All: **Amen!**

Presider: May we rejoice when Christ comes again in glory, giving us eternal life.

All: **Amen!**

Presider: May we be blessed, the Father, and the Son, ✠ and the Holy Spirit.

All: **Amen!**

Dismissal

Presider: Let us go forth as a light to the world as we love and serve the Lord.

All: **Thanks be to God.**

Concluding Song
"Prayer for Peace," CD/CS–#13, mb–#16 or "Walking by Faith," CD/CS–#1, mb–#1

MYSTAGOGY

Mystagogy is the time spent after a service during which the students reflect on their experience. Invite the students to use all their senses to concentrate on the total experience of the service—what they saw, heard, gestured, participated in, sung, and so on. Use the following process:

1. *First have the children close their eyes and remember what happened. You may want to talk through the service yourself and have the children simply remember.*
2. *Have the children tell you what they remember. Use this as a time for brainstorming. Can they reconstruct the service for you and tell you what was important to them?*
3. *Ask them what the liturgy meant to them. Was there something that happened that connected with their own life?*
4. *Ask them to describe how they are feeling or how they felt during the celebration. It is important to go for feeling words—sad, happy, awestruck, confused, and so on. These will facilitate your ability to further the discussion. Ask if any others felt this way.*
5. *Finally, have them ask any question they may have. Understand that you don't have to have all the answers but tell them you will find out the answer, or together you might do some research.*
6. *Close with a prayer from the service and ask the children to remember silently, in their hearts, something very special about this service and how this will affect their relationship with God.*

Liturgy During the Season of Lent

Getting Started

This service is to be celebrated during the Lenten Season. It should also be celebrated during Unit Five. If you study Unit Six during Lent, this liturgy would be appropriate but it is NOT to be used during Holy Week!

During this season we strive for simplicity and an almost stark quality in the ritual—much like our own lives during Lent. Remind students about the traditions of praying and almsgiving. Although fasting is a standard practice of Lent, be very careful when talking with the students about this because issues of food, self-image, and dieting are very serious in our country. Many times a child may use a Church reason for dieting, with the result that eventually there will be health problems.

Familiarize the students with the readings prior to this liturgy. They are rich with images of God's love and our call to adhere to that love. Take time to also reflect on the words of the psalm (91). If you are doing a non-Eucharistic liturgy, also look at the text of the "Canticle of Sirach." This is not a well-known canticle, but its images are rich for the Lenten practice of praying.

If, in your program, you have children preparing for the reception of sacraments on Holy Saturday or Easter Sunday—candidates and catechumens—a prayer is provided that everyone in the entire program can pray over these children. It is very important that everyone in the whole program take part in the journey of our catechumens and candidates.

Keep processions, words, and music as simple as possible. The songs can be easily done a cappella or with just a C instrument obligato or percussion accompaniment. Take time to learn the response for the penitential litany. "Kyrie eleison" and "Christe eleison" are Greek words of praise. We use these terms as shouts to God, proclaiming that Christ is greater than our humanness and should be praised for that.

The "Canticle of Sirach" has a haunting melody and can easily help the children enter into the mystery of the season. A special note about the responsorial psalm: Haas' setting is a delightful adaptation of the Lenten hymn tune "Lonesome Valley." It should be done with a gospel swing and be filled with emotion, yet not move too fast. Listen to the recording for a wonderful interpretation of this. A strong singer in the older grades or even an adult singer would have a good time interpreting the unwritten descant. On the recording the cantor sang from the heart and felt each note. Don't be intimidated. Try it and let the spirit fly with it!

INTRODUCTORY RITES

Opening Song

"Song of the Body of Christ," CD/CS–#18, mb–#24

Greeting

Presider: In the name of the Father, and of the Son, and of the Holy Spirit.

All: **Amen!**

9

| Presider: | The Lord be with you. |
| All: | **And also with you.** |

Or if the presider is a lay minister:

| Presider: | Let us praise our loving God. Blessed be God for ever. |
| All: | **Blessed be God for ever.** |

Opening Comments

Presider: As we gather during this Lenten Season, let us turn to God as we continue to love unconditionally with our hearts, souls, minds, and all our strength.

Penitential Rite

Use the response from the "Penitential Litany" found in the music collection.

Presider: Lord Jesus, you came to show us the way of love and peace.
Cantor sings: Kyrie eleison, followed by all.

Presider: Lord Jesus, you forgive us when we do things that are wrong.
Cantor sings: Christe eleison, followed by all.

Presider: Lord Jesus, you help us as we try and live as people of love and peace.
Cantor sings: Kyrie eleison, followed by all.

| Presider: | May almighty God have mercy on us, forgive us our sins, and bring us to everlasting life. |
| All: | **Amen!** |

Opening Prayer

Presider: Let us pray. *(orans gesture)*
God of all goodness,
you call us to live at peace and to defeat evil with good.
Help us on our Lenten journey as we pray and help those in **need.**
May all our actions praise you as the God who lives and **reigns**
for ever and ever. Amen.

LITURGY OF THE WORD

First Reading

Romans 12:17--18, 21, *Lectionary for Masses with Children, #181*

Responsorial Psalm

"Lord, Be with Me" (Psalm 91), CD/CS–#14, mb–#17
Silence

Gospel Acclamation

Do NOT sing an Alleluia. Instead, use the parish's Lenten Acclamation.

Gospel

Mark 12:28b–31, *Lectionary for Masses with Children*, #182

Homily (Scripture Reflection)

While preparing your homily or reflection, consider these questions:

1. *What lessons from the Scripture have you learned in your own life?*
2. *As reflected in the psalm, what does it mean to live under God's protection and to completely trust in God?*
3. *Who in your life has emulated the two greatest commandments?*
4. *What struggles do you face this Lent, and how can God's love help you through these struggles?*
5. *If your parish is doing RCIA, what have you learned from the catechumens and candidates preparing for Easter?*

Always observe some silence after the homily. If you are doing a Eucharistic liturgy, follow the directives of the Sacramentary from this point on. See notes in the Introduction.

Gospel Canticle *(only use in non-Eucharistic celebrations)*

Presider: Let us stand and sing the words of the prophet Sirach.
Sing "Like the Sweet Fragrance (Canticle of Sirach)," CD/CS–#11, mb–#13

If there are present candidates and catechumens preparing for Holy Saturday or Easter Sunday, instead of singing the canticle, pray the following:

Prayer for Catechumens and Candidates

Presider: I invite those preparing for the Sacraments of Initiation this Easter to come forward, *(name them)* and to kneel before the assembly. I also invite members of their class to come forward and to lay their hands on them as we pray.

Continue after everyone is in position.

God of constant protection,
bless these catechumens and candidates as they
prepare to become full members of our faith this Easter.
May their days be filled with your love and a spirit of understanding.
May the words of Scripture be a light unto their feet.
May we, the community, support them by our prayers so that
we may all celebrate as one Catholic family.
We praise you as the God who lives and reigns for ever and ever.

All: **Amen!**

GENERAL INTERCESSIONS

Use the intercessions with the sung response found in the music collection or use the following, still using a sung response:

Presider: Let us petition God, feeling confident that he hears us and will answer us.

Cantor: *(intones or reads)*
For the Church and all who show us how to live in peace.
Let us pray to the Lord.

For our world and an end to evil which causes war and great harm.
Let us pray to the Lord.

For those who are alone and have lost all self-respect.
Let us pray to the Lord.

Insert your own community's needs here.

For those who are sick and await the healing touch of Christ.
Let us pray to the Lord.

For those who have died and now live in eternal life.
Let us pray to the Lord.

If you are doing a Eucharistic liturgy, proceed to Liturgy of the Eucharist in the Sacramentary and return to this prayer service for the final blessing. If you are not doing a Eucharistic celebration, proceed to the next session.

LORD'S PRAYER

Presider: Let us join in the words that Christ has given us.

All: **Our Father . . . for the kingdom, the power, and the glory are yours, now and for ever. Amen.**

CONCLUDING RITE

"Final Blessing," CD/CS–#19, mb–#25, or:

Blessing
Leader: May almighty God bless us, the Father, and the Son, ✠ and the Holy Spirit.
All: **Amen!**

Dismissal
Leader: Our celebration has ended. Let us go forth to love and serve our God.
All: **Thanks be to God.**

Concluding Song
"Jesus, Heal Us," CD/CS–#16, mb–#20 or "Walking by Faith," CD/CS–#1, mb–#1

Mystagogy

Mystagogy is the time spent after a service during which the students reflect on their experience. Invite the students to use all their senses to concentrate on the total experience of the service—what they saw, heard, gestured, participated in, sung, and so on. Use the following process:

1. First have the children close their eyes and remember what happened. You may want to talk through the service yourself and have the children simply remember.

2. Have the children tell you what they remember. Use this as a time for brainstorming. Can they reconstruct the service for you and tell you what was important to them?

3. Ask them what the liturgy meant to them. Was there something that happened that connected with their own life?

4. Ask them to describe how they are feeling or how they felt during the celebration. It is important to go for feeling words—sad, happy, awestruck, confused, and so on. These will facilitate your ability to further the discussion. Ask if any others felt this way.

5. Finally, have them ask any question they may have. Understand that you don't have to have all the answers but tell them you will find out the answer, or together you might do some research.

6. Close with a prayer from the service and ask the children to remember silently, in their hearts, something very special about this service and how this will affect their relationship with God.

A Community Prayer Service of Forgiveness and Sacrament of Reconciliation

Getting Started

The Sacrament of Reconciliation and a Service of Forgiveness can be two different things. Here they are put together for a reason. There is merit for having children attend a Reconciliation service. Even if they cannot take part in the actual sacrament, they can keep vigil with the rest of the community. By taking part in these services, children will become less inhibited when they can actually take part in the sacrament.

You can celebrate this liturgy any time of the year. Most often parishes celebrate community Reconciliation twice a year. Lent is, of course, the most appropriate time since it is a time of forgiveness and conversion. Another is during the Advent Season. Unfortunately, when doing this during Advent, many children connect Advent with Lent and therefore think of the season of joyful waiting as one of somber repentance. Perhaps a better time would be during the final weeks of the liturgical year. Late October and November would prepare children to begin the new liturgical year—the Advent Season—reconciled to God and with one another.

The service here follows Form II of the Rite of Penance—Rite of Reconciliation of Several Penitents with Individual Confession and Absolution. Please note that individual confessions and absolution take place in the middle of the service. Don't be tempted to skip this part of the service and have individual confessions following the service. It is important to remember that this is a time when the entire group keeps vigil with one another. Music and readings have been provided to be used while students go to confession.

If, for some reason, an ordained presider is unavailable for this service, a lay person may lead the Community Prayer Service of Forgiveness. If you are doing this, use the service as written through Part III: Examination of Conscience. Perhaps have a moment of silence and then proceed to Part V: Proclamation of Praise for God's Mercy and Part VI: Concluding Rite.

Music for the service is simple and should be easily sung by all. Remember that although this is a Reconciliation service, there is a point where the celebration turns into a time of praise and joy—believing that Christ has healed us. Remember this thought when preparing the music. There is to be joy in our praise.

PART I: **INTRODUCTORY** **RITES**	**Opening Song** "Blest Are They," CD/CS–#17, mb–#22
	Greeting
Presider:	Grace, mercy, and peace be with you from God the Father and Christ Jesus our Savior.
All:	**And also with you.**

Or if the presider is a lay minister:

Presider: Blessed be the God of all consolation, who has shown us his great mercy. Blessed be God now and for ever.

All: **Amen.**

Opening Comments

Presider: My children, God calls us to live lives of peace and holiness. Sometimes we have sinned and turned away from God's love. Let us therefore turn to God today and ask for grace and sincere repentance.

Opening Prayer

Presider: Let us pray. *(orans gesture)*
God of love and goodness,
you gave us Christ as a sign of your love.
Christ is our guide to you.
Do not let us act as people who walk in darkness,
but let us walk as children of the light
sharing your love and holiness with all people.
May your light shine through us,
and may we praise you as the God who lives and reigns
for ever and ever. Amen!

PART II: CELEBRATION OF THE WORD OF GOD

First Reading
Ephesians 5:1–2; 8–10, *Lectionary for Masses with Children,* #488–one

Responsorial Psalm
"Lord, Be with Me" (Psalm 91), CD/CS–#14, mb–#17

Gospel Acclamation
"Alleluia/Gospel Acclamation," CD/CS–#5, mb–#5 *(verse 1)*
If this service happens during Lent, do NOT sing the Alleluia. Instead sing the parish Lenten gospel acclamation.

Gospel
Matthew 5:1–12, *Lectionary for Masses with Children,* #512–one

Homily (Scripture Reflection)
While preparing your homily or reflection, consider these questions:
1. *What does it mean to live as "people of light"?*
2. *Which of the Beatitudes speaks to you in your life the most?*
3. *What challenges you in asking for forgiveness in your life?*
4. *When has the Sacrament of Reconciliation helped you in your own life?*
5. *Who in your life shares the peace of reconciliation with you?*

PART III: EXAMINATION OF CONSCIENCE

"Examination of Conscience: Jesus, Heal Us," CD/CS–#16, mb–#20

PART IV: RITE OF RECONCILIATION

General Confession of Sins

Presider: God's covenant, the promise of love, is with us. Having reflected on our lives, we must now come to God and ask forgiveness. Let us kneel and pray.

All: **I confess to almighty God,**
and to you, my brothers and sisters,
that I have sinned through my own fault
in my thoughts and in my words,
in what I have done,
and in what I have failed to do;
and I ask blessed Mary, ever virgin,
all the angels and saints,
and you, my brothers and sisters,
to pray for me to the Lord our God.

Penitential Litany *(found in the music collection)*

Presider: Let us stand.
O God,
you are always with us, even when we are in trouble!
Let us remember your love and kindness.
Be with us as we ask for mercy.

Reader or Cantor: *(All sing Kyrie or Christe eleison after the cantor.)*
1. Give us hearts open to your love. Kyrie eleison.
2. Give us forgiveness from all wrongs. Christe eleison.
3. Give us peace as we admit our guilt. Kyrie eleison.
4. Give us lives of strength as we face evil in the world. Christe eleison.
5. Give us freedom from actions that keep us as prisoners of wrongdoing. Kyrie eleison.
6. Give us strength to obey your call to live lives that are good. Christe eleison.
7. Give us hope when we feel there is no way to ask for forgiveness. Kyrie eleison.
8. Give us light to brighten our way in this world. Christe eleison.

Lord's Prayer

Presider: As one family walking by faith, let us join in the words
Christ himself has given us.

All: Our Father . . . for the kingdom, the power, and the glory are yours, now and for ever. Amen.

Individual Confession and Absolution

During this time it would be appropriate for all present to sing psalms or refrains of repentance. Use "Nothing Can Keep Us from God's Love," found in the music collection and the following Scripture from the Contemporary English Version of the Bible.

1. *Ephesians 3:17b, 19a, 4:1–2, 14b–16*
2. *Ephesians 4:23–24, 5:1–2, 8–10*
3. *Romans 8:31–35, 38–39*

Sing the song twice followed by the reading with soft music. Respond to the reading by singing the song again.

PART V: PROCLAMATION OF PRAISE FOR GOD'S MERCY

The presider asks everyone to stand and sing.
"Everlasting Grace Is Yours" (Psalm 136), mb–#23

A Concluding Prayer of Thanksgiving

Presider: Let us pray. *(orans gesture)*
All-holy and merciful God,
you have shown us the ways of peace and mercy
and you have called us all to become a new creation in you.
May we always walk by faith proclaiming your greatness.
May we shine as lights of love for all the world to see.
We ask this through Christ our Lord. Amen.

PART VI: CONCLUDING RITE

Blessing
"Final Blessing," CD/CS–#19, mb–#25, or:

Solemn Blessing
Presider: May God, our Father, bless us,
for we are his children, born of his mercy.

All: Amen.

Presider: May Christ show us his love and power,
for he died and rose for us.

All: Amen.

Presider: May the Spirit give us peace
and inspire us to live as children of light,
for the love of God lights our hearts.

All: Amen.

Presider: May almighty God bless us, the Father, and the Son, ✠ and the Holy Spirit.

All: **Amen.**

Dismissal

Presider: Go in peace. God has forgiven our sins. Let us walk by faith, singing and praising God.

All: **Thanks be to God.**

Concluding Song

"Prayer for Peace," CD/CS–#13, mb–#16, or "Walking by Faith," CD/CS–#1, mb–#1

MYSTAGOGY

Mystagogy is the time spent after a service during which the students reflect on their experience. Invite the students to use all their senses to concentrate on the total experience of the service—what they saw, heard, gestured, participated in, sung, and so on. Use the following process:

1. *First have the children close their eyes and remember what happened. You may want to talk through the service yourself and have the children simply remember.*
2. *Have the children tell you what they remember. Use this as a time for brainstorming. Can they reconstruct the service for you and tell you what was important to them?*
3. *Ask them what the liturgy meant to them. Was there something that happened that connected with their own life?*
4. *Ask them to describe how they are feeling or how they felt during the celebration. It is important to go for feeling words—sad, happy, awestruck, confused, and so on. These will facilitate your ability to further the discussion. Ask if any others felt this way.*
5. *Finally, have them ask any question they may have. Understand that you don't have to have all the answers but tell them you will find out the answer, or together you might do some research.*
6. *Close with a prayer from the service and ask the children to remember silently, in their hearts, something very special about this service and how this will affect their relationship with God.*

Liturgy for the End of the Catechetical Year

Getting Started

As this is the last school- or parish-wide liturgy, it is a time when we can hopefully relax and enjoy the fruits of all we have accomplished this year. The responses are learned, the readings are rehearsed, and all the ministers are comfortable with what they do.

Prepare the children by going over the previous services with them. Ask them what services they remember the most and what actions or songs they specifically remember.

There are two special actions in this liturgy. During the Introductory Rites we have a sprinkling rite. If this is done during a Eucharistic celebration, it is recommended that this action happen around the parish baptismal font, if it is large enough. Otherwise, bring water from the font in a large bowl to where the children can see the action of the presider moving his or her hand through the water. You will need people to help with the sprinkling rite. Use some catechists or other members of the parish who work in liturgy. Sprinkling branches can be made from "tree fern." Take a bunch of these (around 10) and gather them into a bundle and wrap the bundle with floral wire. Shape the head with scissors. This bundle holds water and can easily be swung for sprinkling.

The other action is the blessing of the students at the end of the liturgy. Gather with the other catechists and devise a procession plan that could best facilitate this action. If the space allows, have the catechists go to the students instead of them coming to you. Mark them with the Sign of the Cross as you pray the words.

If this is a non-Eucharistic service, be sure the water you are using comes from the holy water font in the church. It would still be nice to gather around this font, but sometimes this is not possible. Take special care with this water and remember that it is blessed and holy. The words in the text are appropriate for an ordained or non-ordained minister to pray. These words assume that the water was blessed on Holy Saturday or another appropriate time.

The music for this service are songs the children are familiar with. During this service it is suggested that the refrain of the song (popularly known as the "Celtic Alleluia") be used as the gospel procession, hence connecting the Introductory Rites with the Liturgy of the Word. Even if you are not singing during the Introductory Rites, you may still sing after each of the invocations for the Thanksgiving Over Water Already Blessed. Use an alleluia everyone is familiar with. It is a very weak sign to simply say "alleluia." Always sing this word! Also, listen to the tape for ideas on singing the "Final Blessing." It may be appropriate for the presider and director of religious education to give this blessing. Again, listen to the recording for ideas. There is no formal mystagogy since you may not gather after this liturgy. If you do, follow the process from the previous liturgies, modifying for this occasion.

INTRODUCTORY RITES

Opening Song
"People of God/Alleluia," CD/CS–#8, mb–#8
The presider begins after verse two while the music is still playing.

Greeting

Presider: In the name of the Father, and of the Son, and of the Holy Spirit.
All: **Amen!**

Presider: The Lord be with you.
All: **And also with you.**

Or if the presider is a lay minister:

Presider: Praise be to God, who loves us and fills our lives with joy,
now and for ever.
All: **Amen.**

Opening Comments

Presider: As we gather at the end of this year of religious education, let us look at this time as an ending but also as one of new beginnings.

During this Season of Easter, a season of new beginnings, we remember our Baptism—our birth into life with Christ Jesus.

The presider comes forward and pours water into the font or a large bowl. Other ministers who help with the sprinkling rite then join the presider around the baptismal font (or pool or basin of water).

Thanksgiving Over Water Already Blessed

Presider: Praise to you, God our Creator, you have created water to nourish the land and to quench the thirst of those who are in need of drink.

Cantor: Alleluia!
All: **Alleluia!**

Presider: Praise to you, Christ Jesus. We have been formed as your people, baptized into one family.

Cantor: Alleluia!
All: **Alleluia!**

Presider: Praise to you, Holy Spirit, for calling us from the waters of Baptism to live as children of peace.

Cantor: People of God, rejoice and sing! *All sing refrain of song.*

Sprinkling Rite

Presider and other ministers begin sprinkling the assembly. See "Getting Started" above. During the sprinkling, sing verses three and four of "People of God/Alleluia."

Presider: (*music continues underneath*)
Let us pray.
God of new beginnings,
you have blessed us with a future of hopes and successes.
May our work this past year help us to see your wonders in this world.
We praise you as the God who lives and reigns for ever and ever. Amen.

All sing refrain of song.

LITURGY OF THE WORD

First Reading
Jeremiah 29:11–14
This Scripture is not found in the Lectionary for Masses with Children, but it is very appropriate for the end of the year and can be found in the Contemporary English Version of the Bible.

Responsorial Psalm
"This Is the Day" (Psalm 118), CD/CS–#12, mb–#14

Gospel Acclamation
Refrain of "People of God/Alleluia," CD/CS–#8, mb–#8

Gospel
John 14:23–26, *Lectionary for Masses with Children,* #495–three

Homily (Scripture Reflection)
While preparing your homily or reflection, consider these questions:
  1. *When have you experienced the Father's love in the past year?*
  2. *How does the Spirit lead you in your life?*
  3. *What have you learned in the past year?*
  4. *What do you take with you into the summer?*
  5. *What are your hopes and prayers for the students and teachers?*

Another option here would be to have a neophyte witness to their conversion.

Gospel Canticle (*use only in non-Eucharistic celebrations*)
"Blest Are You, O God" (Canticle of Zachary), CD/CS–#7, mb–#7

GENERAL INTERCESSION

Use the intercessions with the sung response found in the music collection or use the following, still using a sung response:

Presider: Knowing that God hears and answers our prayers, let us present the needs of this day.

Cantor: *(intones or reads)*
For our Church and all who share the faith with us.
Let us pray to the Lord.

For continued peace in our world and in our lives.
Let us pray to the Lord.

For those in our world who are without a home or food.
Let us pray to the Lord.

For the neophytes, the newly baptized, of this parish and in our world.
Let us pray to the Lord.

Insert your own community's needs here.

For those who are sick and are in need of prayers.
Let us pray to the Lord.

Presider: God of hopes and dreams,
your Spirit calls us to be people of peace.
May we walk by faith confident that you are always with us.
We praise you with Christ Jesus, for ever and ever. Amen.

If you are doing a Eucharistic liturgy, proceed to Liturgy of the Eucharist in the Sacramentary and return to this prayer service for the final blessing. If you are not doing a Eucharistic celebration, continue here.

LORD'S PRAYER

Presider: Let us now join in the words Christ himself has given us.

All: **Our Father . . . for the kingdom, the power, and the glory are yours, now and for ever. Amen.**

Sign of Peace

Presider: Lord Jesus Christ, you said to your apostles: I leave you peace, my peace I give you. Look not on our sins but on the faith of your Church, and grant us the peace and unity of your kingdom where you live for ever and ever.

All: **Amen!**

Presider: Let us offer each other the sign of peace.

CONCLUDING RITE

Blessing
"Final Blessing," CD/CS–#19, mb–#25

Presider: Let us bow our heads and ask for God's blessing.

Use the following instead of the blessing prayer found in "Final Blessing."

Loving Creator,
you are our God and we are your people, called by your Spirit.
Shelter and protect us as we share your story and sing your praises.
May you protect and guide us always.
We ask this through Christ our Lord. Amen.

I invite the catechists/teachers to mark each of the students with the Sign of the Cross on the palm of their hands.

The catechists/teachers sign each child saying, "N., may you be blessed, in the name of the Father, and the Son, ✠ and the Holy Spirit. May you be willing to love and serve with God's peace."

Music of "Final Blessing" is played as the catechists sign each student. Sing "Final Blessing" again when all are finished blessing.

Dismissal
Presider: Let us walk by faith, loving and serving our God.
    All: **Thanks be to God.**

Closing Song
"Walking by Faith," CD/CS–#1, mb–#1

Creation

**UNIT 1
CHAPTERS 1–4**

Getting Started

For the Kindergarten year the services are very simple. We gather with a song, a greeting, and an opening prayer. We either have Scripture, ritual action, general intercessions, or a combination of some kind. We conclude with a blessing. These services were written with the intention of each catechist adapting them to the capabilities of the children with whom they are working. The key here is repetition so that the children can learn a flow of ritual. This first service will focus on how God is seen in all of creation. We will use all our senses. Prior to the ritual, prepare some items which incorporate all of the senses: flowers, food, and so on.

**INTRODUCTORY
RITES**

Opening Song

"Alleluia/Gospel Acclamation," CD/CS–#5, mb–#5

Leader: In the name of the Father, and of the Son, and of the Holy Spirit.
All: **Amen!**
Leader: The Lord be with you.
All: **And also with you.**

Opening Comments

Leader: God has given us many things in this world. We thank God for these many gifts.

Opening Prayer

Leader: Let us pray. *(orans gesture)*
God our Father,
we thank you for the world in which we live.
We pray that we can always walk as children who love you.
Help us to always be good to the many gifts you have given us.
We ask this through Christ our Lord. Amen!

language.

**SCRIPTURE
READING**

Wisdom 11:24, 12:1

A Bible should be on the prayer table. Reverence the Bible and then lift and read directly from it.

Leader: A reading from the Book of Wisdom.

God, you created everything, and you love it all. You would never make anything that you did not like. Your eternal Spirit is in everything.

Leader: The word of the Lord.
All: **Thanks be to God.**

Reflection

Share with the children how you look at creation. Talk about how you see God's love in this world.

RITUAL ACTION   *Have the children touch, feel, smell, and hear things of God's creation. When they can identify the object, have them name it and then have everyone say, "We thank you, God, for . . . (name of object)."*

CONCLUDING RITE   "Final Blessing," CD/CS–#19, mb–#25, or:

Leader:	The Lord be with you.
All:	**And also with you.**
Leader:	May almighty God bless us, the Father, the Son, ✠ and the Holy Spirit.
All:	**Amen!**
Leader:	Our celebration has ended. Let us go forth to love and serve our God.
All:	**Thanks be to God.**

Concluding Song
"God's People" (Psalm 100), CD/CS–#2, mb–#2

God

UNIT 2
CHAPTERS 5–8

Getting Started

At this service we focus on the Sign of the Cross and the use of holy water. If possible, pray this service around the holy water font in church. If not, bring some holy water into class and pour it into a large bowl.

INTRODUCTORY RITES

Opening Song

"God's People" (Psalm 100), CD/CS–#2, mb–#2

Leader:	In the name of the Father, and of the Son, and of the Holy Spirit.
All:	**Amen!**
Leader:	The Lord be with you.
All:	**And also with you.**

Opening Comments

Leader: We are a gift from God. Each and every time we enter a church we make the Sign of the Cross, remembering how we belong to God's family.

Opening Prayer

Leader: Let us pray. *(orans gesture)*
God our Father,
you gave us Jesus, your Son, as a special gift to all of us.
May the work of the Spirit be in all our actions.
We always want to praise you as our God.
We ask this through Christ our Lord. Amen!

SCRIPTURE READING

Daniel 12:3

A Bible should be on the prayer table. Reverence the Bible and then lift and read directly from it.

Leader: A reading from the Book of the prophet Daniel.

Everyone who has been wise will shine as bright as the sky above, and everyone who has led others to please God will shine like the stars.

Leader: The word of the Lord.
All: **Thanks be to God.**

Reflection

Talk about how you were called to be a catechist. Discuss how you let the love of God shine in your life.

RITUAL ACTION

Invite each child forward and, using the holy water, mark him or her with a Sign of the Cross. You may want to have the children repeat the action on themselves. State the child's name when marking him or her with water.

Concluding Rite "Final Blessing," CD/CS–#19, mb–#25, or:

Leader: The Lord be with you.
All: **And also with you.**
Leader: May almighty God bless us, the Father, the Son, ✠ and the Holy Spirit.
All: **Amen!**
Leader: Our celebration has ended. Let us go forth to love and serve our God.
All: **Thanks be to God.**

Concluding Song
Refrain of "Walking by Faith," CD/CS–#1, mb–#1

Jesus Christ

UNIT 3
CHAPTERS 9–12

Getting Started

This prayer service is celebrated during the Advent Season. We will talk about Jesus. Bring in many different pictures of Jesus as he may have appeared throughout his life to help the children create a life story about him. For help in finding different images of Jesus, look in art history books. Try to find pictures of Jesus as he is depicted in different cultures.

INTRODUCTORY
RITES

Opening Song
Advent Gathering: "Make Ready the Way," CD/CS–#3, mb–#3

Leader: In the name of the Father, and of the Son, and of the Holy Spirit.
All: **Amen!**
Leader: The Lord be with you.
All: **And also with you.**

Opening Comments
Leader: We are in the Season of Advent. This is a time of waiting. We are waiting for Jesus. Who is this Jesus? Let us take some time to find out about Jesus.

Opening Prayer
Leader: Let us pray. *(orans gesture)*
O God our Father,
you sent Jesus to show us your way of love.
May we always live as children of love.
We ask this through Christ our Lord. Amen!

SCRIPTURE
READING

John 13:34
A Bible should be on the prayer table. Reverence the Bible and then lift and read directly from it.
Leader: The Lord be with you.
All: **And also with you.**
Leader: A reading from the holy Gospel according to John.
All: **Glory to you, O Lord.**

I am giving you a new command. You must love each other, just as I have loved you.

Leader: The gospel of the Lord.
All: **Praise to you, Lord Jesus Christ.**

Reflection
Discuss with the children why God sent Jesus. Show the pictures of Jesus at different ages of his life. Allow the children to ask questions. You may want to take the children for a walk around church to find different images of Jesus. Allow the children to sit with an image for awhile and pray quietly.

RITUAL ACTION

If you have an Advent wreath or can gather around the one in church, use the Blessing of the Advent Wreath found on the CD/CS–#3, "Advent Gathering." You may also wish to invite someone from the parish staff or liturgy team to join you in church and pray the blessing that was used to bless the parish Advent wreath.

CONCLUDING RITE

"Final Blessing," CD/CS–#19, mb–#25, or:

Leader: The Lord be with you.
All: **And also with you.**
Leader: May almighty God bless us, the Father, the Son, ✠ and the Holy Spirit.
All: **Amen!**
Leader: Our celebration has ended. Let us go forth to love and serve our God.
All: **Thanks be to God.**

Concluding Song
"Prayer for Peace," CD/CS–#13, mb–#16

The Church

UNIT 4
CHAPTERS 13–16

Getting Started

During the Season of Christmas, children need to be challenged to think of others. Ritually, this can be done by asking the children to pray for others in the general intercessions. Take time prior to the ritual to talk about people who are in need of our prayers this season. Again, pictures may help the children think more globally.

INTRODUCTORY
RITES

Opening Song

"God's People" (Psalm 100), CD/CS–#2, mb–#2

Leader: In the name of the Father, and of the Son, and of the Holy Spirit.
All: **Amen!**
Leader: The Lord be with you.
All: **And also with you**.

Opening Comments

Leader: During the Season of Christmas, we remember to pray for many people. Jesus came as a very poor child to show us how to love ALL people.

Opening Prayer

Leader: Let us pray. *(orans gesture)*
God of love and light,
thank you for the gift of Jesus.
He came to show us how to love all people.
May we always love others as you have loved us.
We ask this through Christ our Lord. Amen!

SCRIPTURE
READING

Ephesians 2:19b, 22

A Bible should be on the prayer table. Reverence the Bible and then lift and read directly from it.

Leader: A reading from the Letter to the Ephesians.

You are citizens with everyone else who belongs to the family of God. And you are part of that building Christ has built as a place for God's own Spirit to live.

Leader: The word of the Lord.
All: **Thanks be to God.**

Reflection

Discuss what the Season of Christmas means to you. Talk about belonging to the family of God and how we are responsible for praying for all people.

INTERCESSIONS   "General Intercessions," in music collection or:

Leader: Knowing that God loves us and hears us, let us come to God with our prayers.

For all those people who show us how to love God.
Let us pray to the Lord.

All: **Lord, hear our prayer.**

Leader: For people who keep our world safe from bad things.
Let us pray to the Lord.

For people who have no home and are without food.
Let us pray to the Lord.

For things we want to pray about. *(Insert your own intentions here.)*
Let us pray to the Lord.

For those who are sick, especially . . . *(name people)*.
Let us pray to the Lord.

God of all love
You have promised to be with us always.
Hear our prayers.
Answer them as you feel they should be answered.
We ask this through Christ our Lord. Amen.

CONCLUDING RITE   "Final Blessing," CD/CS–#19, mb–#25, or:

Leader: The Lord be with you.
All: **And also with you.**
Leader: May almighty God bless us, the Father, the Son, ✠ and the Holy Spirit.
All: **Amen!**
Leader: Our celebration has ended. Let us go forth to love and serve our God.
All: **Thanks be to God.**

Concluding Song
"Alleluia/Gospel Acclamation," CD/CS–#5, mb–#5

Christian Morality

UNIT 5
CHAPTERS 17–20

Getting Started

During this celebration we look at times when we have made wrong choices. When we have made wrong choices, we have hurt others and even hurt our relationship with God. Again, connect these ideas with what is going on in the children's lives. Prior to the session you could have the children role-play good and bad choices.

INTRODUCTORY
RITES

Opening Song

"Lord, Be with Me" (Psalm 91), CD/CS–#14, mb–#17

Leader: In the name of the Father, and of the Son, and of the Holy Spirit.
All: **Amen!**
Leader: The Lord be with you.
All: **And also with you.**

Opening Comments

Leader: We make choices between what is right and what is wrong. When we choose the wrong way, we must remember to turn to Jesus. Jesus will help us find the right way.

Opening Prayer

Leader: Let us pray. *(orans gesture)*
Loving God,
you gave us Jesus to show us how to live as good children.
Sometimes we do things that are wrong.
Forgive us for not loving others as we should.
Help us to be better people.
We ask this through Christ our Lord. Amen!

SCRIPTURE
READING

Luke 6:27a, 31

A Bible should be on the prayer table. Reverence the Bible and then lift and read directly from it.

Leader: The Lord be with you.
All: **And also with you.**
Leader: A reading from the holy Gospel according to Luke.
All: **Glory to you, O Lord.**

This is what I say to all who will listen to me: Treat others just as you want to be treated.

Leader: The gospel of the Lord.
All: **Praise to you, Lord Jesus Christ.**

Reflection

Tell of a time in your life when you had to love an enemy. Share what that felt like. Share what it means to ask forgiveness and how you must humble yourself. Speak about how God is part of forgiving others.

INTERCESSIONS "General Intercessions," in music collection or:

Leader: Let us come before God asking for forgiveness.

For times we did not follow those who showed us how to live as children of God. Let us pray to the Lord.

All: **Lord, hear our prayer.**

Leader: For times we didn't help others who wanted help. Let us pray to the Lord.

For times we didn't care about other people. Let us pray to the Lord.

For times we were afraid to help a friend in need. Let us pray to the Lord.

Let us think about times in our own life when we have done something wrong.

God of love, we are truly sorry for hurting others. We know that when we hurt others, we hurt you. Help us not to do this again. We ask this through Christ our Lord. Amen.

CONCLUDING RITE "Final Blessing," CD/CS–#19, mb–#25, or:

Leader: The Lord be with you.
All: **And also with you.**
Leader: May almighty God bless us, the Father, the Son, ✠ and the Holy Spirit.
All: **Amen!**
Leader: Our celebration has ended. Let us go forth to love and serve our God.
All: **Thanks be to God.**

Concluding Song

"Prayer for Peace," CD/CS–#13, mb–#16

The Sacraments

**UNIT 6
CHAPTERS 21–24**

Getting Started

During this service we reflect on the cross on which Jesus died. Talk about how Jesus died on the cross and then was raised to new life by God the Father. We celebrate the beauty of the cross as a sign of how Christ died on Good Friday and was raised to new life on Easter.

INTRODUCTORY RITES

Opening Song

"Song of the Body of Christ," CD/CS–#18, mb–#24

Leader: In the name of the Father, and of the Son, and of the Holy Spirit.
All: **Amen!**
Leader: The Lord be with you.
All: **And also with you.**

Opening Comments

Leader: As children who follow Christ, we make the Sign of the Cross on ourselves. We see many crosses in our lives. Let us take some time to think about what the cross of Jesus really means.

Opening Prayer

Leader: Let us pray. *(orans gesture)*
God our Father,
Jesus your Son died on the cross to save us.
The cross must have been very heavy to carry.
Help us to carry our crosses,
even if that means having to do things we sometimes don't like to do.
We know you will help us with our crosses.
We ask this through Christ our Lord. Amen!

SCRIPTURE READING

Philippians 2:6, 8–9

A Bible should be on the prayer table. Reverence the Bible and then lift and read directly from it.

Leader: A reading from the Letter of Paul to the Philippians.

Christ was truly God. But he did not try to remain equal with God. Christ was humble. He obeyed God and even died on a cross. Then God gave Christ the highest place and honored his name above all others.

Leader: The word of the Lord.
All: **Thanks be to God.**

Reflection

Discuss what the cross means to you and why the cross of Jesus is different than other crosses. Discuss why Jesus died on the cross and how he is now honored. You may want to discuss how this fits into Holy Week. Don't forget to mention that God the Father raised Jesus from the dead!

RITUAL ACTION

Find as many crosses as possible. Wander around singing "Song of the Body of Christ" and see where there are crosses in your classroom, building, church, or home. If possible, stop at the church and have someone explain the parish cross to you. Why was this cross chosen for this church? Have the entire class bow before the parish cross in silence. Then sing the refrain of "Song of the Body of Christ" again.

CONCLUDING RITE

"Final Blessing," CD/CS–#19, mb–#25, or:

Leader:	The Lord be with you.
All:	**And also with you.**
Leader:	May almighty God bless us, the Father, the Son, ✠ and the Holy Spirit.
All:	**Amen!**
Leader:	Our celebration has ended. Let us go forth to love and serve our God.
All:	**Thanks be to God.**

Concluding Song

"Deep Down I Know," CD/CS–#10, mb–#12

Salvation History

Getting Started

Reflect on past services of the year. Think about how your students have changed, and celebrate their moving into first grade. You have been their catechist and their guide. This ritual works well when done around the Easter baptismal font. If you are gathering somewhere else, bring holy water from the church and pour it into a large bowl so that the children can see you dip your hand in when you bless them.

INTRODUCTORY
RITES

Opening Song

"Alleluia/Gospel Acclamation," CD/CS–#5, mb–#5

Leader:	In the name of the Father, and of the Son, and of the Holy Spirit.
All:	**Amen!**
Leader:	The Lord be with you.
All:	**And also with you.**

Opening Comments

Leader: As we come to the end of a school year, we must prepare ourselves to move on. We take with us what we have learned about God, Jesus, and the Holy Spirit. We will always try to live as children of God.

Opening Prayer

Leader: Let us pray. *(orans gesture)*
God of all wonderful things and our Father,
you raised Jesus from the dead
so that we could see how wonderful you are.
Help us always walk by faith.
We ask this through Christ our Lord. Amen!

SCRIPTURE
READING

1 Corinthians 2:9–10

A Bible should be on the prayer table. Reverence the Bible and then lift and read directly from it.

Leader: A reading from the First Letter of Paul to the Corinthians.

It is just as the Scriptures say, "What God has planned for people who love him is more than eyes have seen or ears have heard. It has never even entered our minds!" God's Spirit has shown you everything. His Spirit finds out everything, even what is deep in the mind of God.

Leader:	The word of the Lord.
All:	**Thanks be to God.**

Reflection

Share your feelings about the past year. What have you learned about God? Discuss with the children all that they have seen and heard. Connect this to the fact that there is even more to learn. We must always trust in God. Share your faith story and your prayers for each student. Name each child and tell something good about him or her.

RITUAL ACTION   *Invite each child to come forward to the holy water. Explain that this water is used at Baptism. Sign each child saying: "N., may you always live as a new creation of Jesus. Amen."*

INTERCESSIONS   "General Intercessions," in music collection or:

Leader: Let us come before God with our needs.

    For all who lead us in faith. Let us pray to the Lord.
All: **Lord, hear our prayer.**

Leader: For all who keep our world a place of peace.
    Let us pray to the Lord.

    For those who are without food or without homes.
    Let us pray to the Lord.

    Let us add our own prayers now. *(Insert their needs here.)*
    Let us pray to the Lord.

    For those who are sick. Let us pray to the Lord.

    Let us pray.
    O God our Father,
    may we always come to you with our needs.
    We pray knowing that you hear us.
    Help us as we go forth from this class.
    May we always live as children of peace and love.
    We ask this through Christ our Lord. Amen!

CONCLUDING RITE   "Final Blessing," CD/CS–#19, mb–#25, or:

Leader: The Lord be with you.
All: **And also with you.**
Leader: May almighty God bless us, the Father, the Son, ✠ and the Holy Spirit.
All: **Amen!**
Leader: Our celebration has ended. Let us go forth to love and serve our God.
All: **Thanks be to God.**

Concluding Song
"Walking by Faith," CD/CS–#1, mb–#1

God's Creation

UNIT 1
CHAPTERS 1–4

Getting Started

Throughout this year we will be having very simple celebrations. The prayer services consist of an opening song, a greeting, a Scripture/ritual action, and some kind of conclusion. Feel free to modify the prayers to fit the ability of your students. Always look at the service prior to praying to see if there are any responses that need to be reviewed with the children. During this first service the focus is on God creating the world. When you do the litany, you may want to have tangible things the children can see or touch. Bring in pictures of special people and places and have the children do the same.

INTRODUCTORY
RITES

Opening Song

"God's People" (Psalm 100), CD/CS–#2, mb–#2

Leader: In the name of the Father, and of the Son, and of the Holy Spirit.
All: **Amen!**
Leader: The Lord be with you.
All: **And also with you.**

Opening Comments

Leader: The world God made is filled with many wonderful things. Let us take some time to say "thank you" to God for all the things in our world.

Opening Prayer

Leader: Let us pray. *(orans gesture)*
Thank you, God, for your gifts of love.
You made the trees and rocks and seas and sun above.
Thank you, God, for our world so bright.
We will sing our thanks to you every day and night.
We ask this through Christ our Lord. Amen!

SCRIPTURE
READING

Genesis 1:31, 2:1

A Bible should be on the prayer table. Reverence the Bible and then lift and read directly from it.

Leader: A reading from the Book of Genesis.

God looked at what he had done. All of it was very good! Evening came and then morning—that was the sixth day. So the heavens and the earth and everything else were created.

Leader: The word of the Lord.
All: **Thanks be to God.**

Reflection

Share with the group your feelings about the Scripture reading. Use these questions for your personal reflection.

1. *What in the world is truly special to you?*
2. *How do you see God's love in the world around you?*

RITUAL ACTION *During this ritual you can show the children photographs or pictures, or you can walk with the children around the classroom. Show them something and say the following:*

Leader: What is this?

A child: *(tells you what it is)*

Leader: Let us thank God for the gift of . . . *(Say the name of the item—perhaps "a baby," "my family," "a tree," "my pet," and so on.)*

All: **Thank you, God, for this gift. Amen.**

CONCLUDING RITE "Final Blessing," CD/CS–#19, mb–#25, or:

Leader: The Lord be with you.

All: **And also with you.**

Leader: May almighty God bless us, the Father, the Son, ✠ and the Holy Spirit.

All: **Amen!**

Leader: Our celebration has ended. Let us go forth to love and serve our God.

All: **Thanks be to God.**

Concluding Song

"Deep Down I Know," CD/CS–#10, mb–#12

The Holy Trinity

Getting Started

During this prayer service we will focus on the text of the Lord's Prayer. Review the text slowly with the children and perhaps even have it printed on a large poster. You may want to practice the prayer with some of the students' family members in the room. Have them help the children. Another option would be to attend a parish liturgy as a group and listen for when the assembly prays the Lord's Prayer.

INTRODUCTORY
RITES

Opening Song
"Walking by Faith," CD/CS–#1, mb–#1

Leader: In the name of the Father, and of the Son, and of the Holy Spirit.
All: **Amen!**
Leader: The Lord be with you.
All: **And also with you.**

Opening Comments

Leader: Jesus taught everyone how to pray. He told us to pray to his Father in heaven. Together we will pray that prayer. It will be a part of many prayers throughout our lives.

Opening Prayer

Leader: Let us pray. *(orans gesture)*
God our Father,
you gave us your Son, Jesus, who was a teacher.
May we learn from him.
May we live as children who always pray to you.
We ask this through Christ our Lord. Amen!

SCRIPTURE
READING

Matthew 6:7–8

A Bible should be on the prayer table. Reverence the Bible and then lift and read directly from it.

Leader: The Lord be with you.
All: **And also with you.**
Leader: A reading from the holy Gospel according to Matthew.
All: **Glory to you, O Lord.**

When you pray, don't talk on and on as people do who don't know God. They think God likes to hear long prayers. Don't be like them. Your Father knows what you need before you ask.

Leader: The gospel of the Lord.
All: **Praise to you, Lord Jesus Christ.**

Reflection

Share with the group your feelings about the Scripture reading. Use these questions for your personal reflection.

1. *What prayers are important to you?*
2. *When do you use prayer in your life?*
3. *Who taught you to pray?*

LORD'S PRAYER

Leader: Let us join in the words that Christ has given us.

All: **Our Father . . . for the kingdom, the power, and the glory are yours, now and for ever. Amen.**

CONCLUDING RITE

"Final Blessing," CD/CS–#19, mb–#25, or:

Leader: The Lord be with you.
All: **And also with you.**
Leader: May almighty God bless us, the Father, the Son, ✠ and the Holy Spirit.
All: **Amen!**
Leader: Our celebration has ended. Let us go forth to love and serve our God.
All: **Thanks be to God.**

Concluding Song

"God's People" (Psalm 100), CD/CS–#2, mb–#2

Jesus, the Son of God

UNIT 3
CHAPTERS 9–12

Getting Started

This prayer service focuses on the general intercessions. If you want to have a sung response, you can use the general intercessions found in the music collection. If not, use the intercessions shown here. This will be a time to allow the children to ask or pray to God for anything. Prior to the prayer you may want to have the children talk about what they would pray to God for and about. You may even wish to have someone from the parish who writes the general intercessions come in and talk to the children about the way these prayers are prepared. Another starting point may be to bring in a newspaper and ask the children if they know about events that are happening in the world. See if any of these are things the group could pray about.

INTRODUCTORY RITES

Opening Song

"To You, O Lord" (Psalm 25), CD/CS–#6, mb–#6

Leader:	In the name of the Father, and of the Son, and of the Holy Spirit.
All:	**Amen!**
Leader:	The Lord be with you.
All:	**And also with you.**

Opening Comments

Leader: We know that God will answer our prayers. Today we come to God with prayers that we have made up. They come from our hearts and our minds.

Opening Prayer

Leader: Let us pray. *(orans gesture)*
O God,
you are our loving and true God.
We love you with all our heart, soul, and strength.
May we always come to you in honesty.
May we trust in your love for us.
We ask this through Christ our Lord. Amen!

SCRIPTURE READING

Matthew 19:13–15

A Bible should be on the prayer table. Reverence the Bible and then lift and read directly from it.

Leader:	The Lord be with you.
All:	**And also with you.**
Leader:	A reading from the holy Gospel according to Matthew.
All:	**Glory to you, O Lord.**

Some people brought their children to Jesus, so that he could place his hands on them and pray for them. His disciples told the people to stop bothering him. But Jesus said, "Let the children come to me, and don't try to stop them! People who are like these children belong to God's kingdom." After Jesus had placed his hands on the children, he left.

Leader: The gospel of the Lord.

All: **Praise to you, Lord Jesus Christ.**

Reflection

Share with the group your feelings about the Scripture reading. Use these questions for your personal reflection.

1. *What would it have been like to be held by Jesus?*
2. *When have you been like a child of God in your prayers?*
3. *How can you be like Christ to all of God's children?*

INTERCESSIONS "General Intercessions," in music collection or:

Leader: Let us come before God with our needs.

For all people who teach us about God. Let us pray to the Lord.

All: **Lord, hear our prayer.**

Leader: For people who take care of the world we live in. Let us pray to the Lord.

For people who don't have homes or food. Let us pray to the Lord.

What other things would you like to pray for?

Insert your own intentions here.

For those who are sick, especially. . . *(name them here)*. Let us pray to the Lord.

For those who have died and now live in heaven with Jesus. Let us pray to the Lord.

LORD'S PRAYER

Leader: Let us join in the words that Christ has given us.

All: **Our Father . . . for the kingdom, the power, and the glory are yours, now and for ever. Amen.**

CONCLUDING RITE   "Final Blessing," CD/CS–#19, mb–#25, or:

Leader:	The Lord be with you.
All:	**And also with you.**
Leader:	May almighty God bless us, the Father, the Son, ✠ and the Holy Spirit.
All:	**Amen!**
Leader:	Our celebration has ended. Let us go forth to love and serve our God.
All:	**Thanks be to God.**

Concluding Song
"Prayer for Peace," CD/CS–#13, mb–#16

God's Church

Getting Started

This prayer service is to be celebrated during the Christmas Season. For the ritual action, use the custom of having the children put straw into a manger when the they state an act of service they have performed. This will encourage them to think of things they can do for other people. Helping at home, giving money to the bell ringers of the Salvation Army, being a very good friend, or giving mittens or clothes to children who don't have any are things the children could do. See if the class can adopt a family for whom they can buy or give food. Have the children come up with a menu and see which items they can bring from home. Include family members in this activity.

INTRODUCTORY RITES

Opening Song
"Prayer for Peace," CD/CS–#13, mb–#16

Leader: In the name of the Father, and of the Son, and of the Holy Spirit.
All: **Amen!**
Leader: The Lord be with you.
All: **And also with you.**

Opening Comments
Leader: We are called to love everyone. In this Season of Christmas we hear about so many people getting so many things. Let's take time and think about things we can GIVE other people.

Opening Prayer
Leader: Let us pray. *(orans gesture)*
God of all love,
your Son Jesus told us to love each other as brothers and sisters.
May we never give up in loving others.
May we never stop praying to you.
May we always take care of your people who are in need.
We ask this through Christ our Lord. Amen!

SCRIPTURE READING

Romans 12:10–13
A Bible should be on the prayer table. Reverence the Bible and then lift and read directly from it.
Leader: A reading from the Letter of Paul to the Romans.

Love each other as brothers and sisters and honor others more than you do yourself. Never give up. Eagerly follow the Holy Spirit and serve the Lord. Let your hope make you glad. Be patient in time of trouble and never stop praying. Take care of God's needy people and welcome strangers into your home.

Leader: The word of the Lord.
All: **Thanks be to God.**

Reflection
Share with the group your feelings about the Scripture reading. Use these questions for your personal reflection.
1. *Who are God's people who are in need in this world?*
2. *How can we help them?*
3. *When have you helped someone and known you got the strength from God?*
4. *Who are people in this world who help other people?*

RITUAL ACTION

Look at "Getting Started" above. This might be a time to have the children state their act of service as they put straw in the manger. Or you might want to do a ritual procession of items for the family (families) you may be helping this Christmas Season. Sing a familiar Christmas song at this time.

LORD'S PRAYER

Leader: Let us join in the words that Christ has given us.

All: **Our Father . . . for the kingdom, the power, and the glory are yours, now and for ever. Amen.**

CONCLUDING RITE

"Final Blessing," CD/CS–#19, mb–#25, or:

Leader: The Lord be with you.
All: **And also with you.**
Leader: May almighty God bless us, the Father, the Son, ✠ and the Holy Spirit.
All: **Amen!**
Leader: Our celebration has ended. Let us go forth to love and serve our God.
All: **Thanks be to God.**

Concluding Song
"Walking by Faith," CD/CS–#1, mb–#1

Living God's Love

Getting Started

During this service we will have an examination of conscience. Although this may seem difficult for children, the one recorded on the CD and cassette is quite effective in helping children look at the choices they make in their life. They simply need to learn the refrain of "Jesus, Heal Us," CD/CS–#16.

INTRODUCTORY
RITES

Opening Song

"Lord, Be with Me" (Psalm 91), CD/CS–#14, mb–#17

Leader:	In the name of the Father, and of the Son, and of the Holy Spirit.
All:	**Amen!**
Leader:	The Lord be with you.
All:	**And also with you.**

Opening Comments

Leader: We all have to learn to be sorry when we do something wrong. Let us remember, though, that God loves us no matter what! God is always willing to forgive us.

Opening Prayer

Leader: Let us pray. *(orans gesture)*
We thank you,
God our Father.
You made us to live for you and for each other.
We can see and speak to one another,
and become friends,
and share our joys and sorrows.
Help all who follow Jesus
to work for peace
and to bring happiness to others.
We ask this through Christ our Lord. Amen!

SCRIPTURE
READING

Mark 12:28–31

A Bible should be on the prayer table. Reverence the Bible and then lift and read directly from it.

Leader:	The Lord be with you.
All:	**And also with you.**
Leader:	A reading from the holy Gospel according to Mark.
All:	**Glory to you, O Lord.**

One of the teachers of the Law of Moses came up while Jesus and the Sadducees were arguing. When he heard Jesus give a good answer, he asked him, "What is the most important commandment?" Jesus answered, "The most important one says: 'People of Israel, you have only one Lord and God. You must love him with all your heart, soul, mind, and strength.' The second most important commandment says: 'Love others as much as you love yourself.' No other commandment is more important than these."

Leader: The gospel of the Lord.
All: **Praise to you, Lord Jesus Christ.**

Reflection

Share with the group your feelings about the Scripture reading. Use these questions for your personal reflection.
1. *What does it mean to love God with "all your heart, soul, mind, and strength"?*
2. *How do you live these two important commandments?*
3. *Why can it be hard for you to apologize for something wrong you have done?*

RITUAL ACTION

Use "Examination of Conscience: Jesus, Heal Us," CD/CS–#16, mb–#20. When asked to kneel, do not have students pray the Confiteor. Instead, pray the words on page 119 in the student's textbook or simply pray the third option of the Penitential Rite–"Lord, have mercy. Christ, have mercy. Lord, have mercy."

LORD'S PRAYER
Leader: Let us join in the words that Christ has given us.

All: **Our Father . . . for the kingdom, the power, and the glory are yours, now and for ever. Amen.**

CONCLUDING RITE

"Final Blessing," CD/CS–#19, mb–#25, or:

Leader: The Lord be with you.
All: **And also with you.**
Leader: May almighty God bless us, the Father, the Son, ✠ and the Holy Spirit.
All: **Amen!**
Leader: Our celebration has ended. Let us go forth to love and serve our God.
All: **Thanks be to God.**

Concluding Song
"Prayer for Peace," CD/CS–#13, mb–#16

Signs of God's Love

Getting Started

During this prayer service we will prepare and sit at a table for ritual. You may want to have some children bring dishes from home, or you can provide the needed items for the table. Have the children prepare the table before they sit down at it. It is important that you take time to let the children set the table. What would they want on this table—flowers, napkins, just forks, just spoons? It is their table, how would they dress it? You will also need one loaf of bread that you can break easily and share with the children. Check to see if any of the children have any food allergies that would prevent them from participating in this ritual.

INTRODUCTORY RITES

Opening Song

"The Bread That Gives Life," CD/CS–#9, mb–#10

Leader: In the name of the Father, and of the Son, and of the Holy Spirit.
All: **Amen!**
Leader: The Lord be with you.
All: **And also with you.**

Opening Comments

Leader: Before Jesus died and was raised from the dead, he gathered with his apostles for a final meal. At that meal he gave thanks and praise.

Opening Prayer

Leader: Let us pray. *(orans gesture)*
God our Father,
you have brought us here together
so that we can give you thanks and praise
for all the wonderful things you have done.
May our actions always tell the world
how much you love us and care for us.
We ask this through Christ our Lord. Amen!

SCRIPTURE READING

Ephesians 1:4, 6

A Bible should be on the prayer table. Reverence the Bible and then lift and read directly from it.

Leader: A reading from the Letter to the Ephesians.

Before the world was created, God had Christ choose us to live with him and to be his holy and innocent and loving people. God was very kind to us because of the Son he dearly loves, and so we should praise God.

Leader: The word of the Lord.
All: **Thanks be to God.**

Reflection

Share with the group your feelings about the Scripture reading. Use these questions for your personal reflection.

1. *What does it mean to be chosen by God?*
2. *Why did God give us his Son?*
3. *Is there anyone in your life who communicates the love of Christ to you?*

RITUAL ACTION

Have the children set the table. See notes above. When all the children are seated, sit with them and begin to break a loaf of bread. As you hold a piece of bread, say what you are thankful for. Then have the children do the same. After all the children have said what they are thankful for, everyone may eat the bread.

LORD'S PRAYER

Leader: Let us join in the words that Christ has given us.

All: **Our Father . . . for the kingdom, the power, and the glory are yours, now and for ever. Amen.**

CONCLUDING RITE

"Final Blessing," CD/CS–#19, mb–#25, or:

Leader: The Lord be with you.
All: **And also with you.**
Leader: May almighty God bless us, the Father, the Son, ✠ and the Holy Spirit.
All: **Amen!**
Leader: Our celebration has ended. Let us go forth to love and serve our God.
All: **Thanks be to God.**

Concluding Song
"Song of the Body of Christ," CD/CS–#18, mb–#24

God Saves Us

UNIT 7
CHAPTERS 25–28

Getting Started

As the catechetical year comes to an end, take time to review where you have been this year. Review highlights of each of the seven prayer rituals. This ritual works well when done around the Easter baptismal font. If possible, gather around the parish font. If not, bring holy water from church and pour it into a large bowl, light a candle, and gather.

INTRODUCTORY RITES

Opening Song

"Alleluia/Gospel Acclamation," CD/CS–#5, mb–#5

Leader: In the name of the Father, and of the Son, and of the Holy Spirit.
All: **Amen!**
Leader: The Lord be with you.
All: **And also with you.**

Opening Comments

Leader: As we come to the end of another year, we come to the waters of New Life. These waters are used for Baptism. We are all new creations because God the Father loves us and gave us his Son, Jesus.

Opening Prayer

Leader: Let us pray. *(orans gesture)*
Holy and ever-living God and Father,
you raised Jesus from the dead
so that we all may live in freedom.
May we always walk by faith.
May we serve, with love, all those in need.
We ask this through Christ our Lord. Amen!

SCRIPTURE READING

Romans 8:38–39

A Bible should be on the prayer table. Reverence the Bible and then lift and read directly from it.

Leader: A reading from the Letter of Paul to the Romans.

I am sure that nothing can separate us from God's love—not life or death, not angels or spirits, not the present or the future, and not powers above or powers below. Nothing in all creation can separate us from God's love for us in Christ Jesus our Lord!

Leader: The word of the Lord.
All: **Thanks be to God.**

Reflection

Share with the group your feelings about the Scripture reading. Use these questions for your personal reflection.

1. *When have you felt God's love the strongest?*
2. *How has God's love been shown to you this year?*
3. *What mission of love will you take forth into the world?*

RITUAL ACTION *Use "Greeting and Thanksgiving Over Water Already Blessed" found in "People of God/Alleluia," CD/CS–#8, mb–#8, or the following:*

Leader: God our Father,
you give us grace through special signs,
which tell us of the wonders of your power.
Please respond, "Blessed are you, O Lord our God!"
Move your hand through the water during the invocations. You may also want to have the students move their hands through the water during their response.

When the world was created you gave us water to quench our thirst. *Response.*

You moved the waters of the Red Sea so your followers could escape from people who would try to kill them. *Response.*

You had Jesus baptized by John in the water of the Jordan River. *Response.*

And you call us all to the waters in our Baptism. *Response.*

I invite everyone to come forward and sign themselves with these waters.
The leader blesses himself or herself making the Sign of the Cross with the holy water and then the students do the same.

LORD'S PRAYER
Leader: Let us join in the words that Christ has given us.

All: **Our Father . . . for the kingdom, the power, and the glory are yours, now and for ever. Amen.**

CONCLUDING RITE   "Final Blessing," CD/CS–#19, mb–#25, or:

Leader: The Lord be with you.
All: **And also with you.**
Leader: May almighty God bless us, the Father, the Son, ✠ and the Holy Spirit.
All: **Amen!**
Leader: Our celebration has ended. Let us go forth to love and serve our God.
All: **Thanks be to God.**

Concluding Song
"Walking by Faith," CD/CS–#1, mb–#1

God's Gift to Our World

**UNIT 1
CHAPTERS 1–4**

Getting Started

As we celebrate this year, we reflect on Jesus, present in Scripture, music, and the symbols of earth, air, fire, and water.

**INTRODUCTORY
RITES**

Opening Song

"Walking by Faith," CD/CS–#1, mb–#1 *(Review refrain.)*

Leader: In the name of the Father, and of the Son, and of the Holy Spirit.
All: **Amen!**
Leader: The Lord be with you.
All: **And also with you.**

Opening Comments

Leader: As we gather this year, we remember how Jesus loves each and everyone of us.

Opening Prayer

Leader: Let us pray. *(orans gesture)*
Dear God,
you made us.
You call us to grow in love,
and you sent your Son, Jesus, to show us how.
Thank you for giving us people to care for us,
as Joseph and Mary cared for Jesus.
Help our families to be holy families, too.
We ask this through Christ our Lord. Amen!

**SCRIPTURE
READING**

John 3:16–17

A Bible should be on the prayer table. Reverence the Bible and then lift and read directly from it.

Leader: The Lord be with you.
All: **And also with you.**
Leader: A reading from the holy Gospel according to John.
All: **Glory to you, O Lord.**

God loved the people of this world so much that he gave his only Son, so that everyone who has faith in him will have eternal life and never really die. God did not send his Son into the world to condemn its people. He sent him to save them!

Leader: The gospel of the Lord.
All: **Praise to you, Lord Jesus Christ.**

Reflection

Share with the group your feelings about the Scripture reading. Use these questions for your personal reflection.

1. *Who is Jesus for you?*
2. *When have you felt Jesus' love?*
3. *What is your wish for your children this year?*

LORD'S PRAYER   *(Review the Lord's Prayer slowly.)*

Leader: Let us join in the words that Christ has given us.

All: **Our Father . . . for the kingdom, the power, and the glory are yours, now and for ever. Amen.**

CONCLUDING RITE   "Final Blessing," CD/CS–#19, mb–#25, or:

Leader: The Lord be with you.

All: **And also with you.**

Leader: May almighty God bless us, the Father, the Son, ✠ and the Holy Spirit.

All: **Amen!**

Leader: Our celebration has ended. Let us go forth to love and serve our God.

All: **Thanks be to God.**

Concluding Song

"Walking by Faith," CD/CS–#1, mb–#1

Jesus Teaches Us about God

UNIT 2
CHAPTERS 5–8

Getting Started

You will need holy water for this ritual. If possible, gather around the parish baptismal font or bring holy water from the church and pour it in a large bowl. It is important for the children to be able to touch the water and for you to sign each child with the water as you say his or her name.

INTRODUCTORY RITES

Opening Song

"Alleluia/Gospel Acclamation," CD/CS–#5, mb–#5

Leader: In the name of the Father, and of the Son, and of the Holy Spirit.
All: **Amen!**
Leader: The Lord be with you.
All: **And also with you.**

Opening Comments

Leader: Jesus loves us so much. There have been people before us who loved and followed Jesus. They are called saints. Do any of you know any saints?
Leave time to discuss or share the story of your favorite saint.

Opening Prayer

Leader: Let us pray. *(orans gesture)*
God our Creator,
Jesus taught us to call you our Father.
Jesus Christ, Son of the Father,
you promised to send the Holy Spirit to your friends.
May the Spirit always be with us in your Church.
We ask this through Christ our Lord. Amen!

SCRIPTURE READING

Ephesians 3:7–8

A Bible should be on the prayer table. Reverence the Bible and then lift and read directly from it.

Leader: A reading from the Letter to the Ephesians.

God treated me with kindness. His power worked in me, and it became my job to spread the good news. I am the least important of all God's people. But God was kind and chose me to tell the Gentiles that because of Christ there are blessings that cannot be measured.

Leader: The word of the Lord.
All: **Thanks be to God.**

Reflection
Share with the group your feelings about the Scripture reading. Use these questions for your personal reflection.

1. *Share why you were called to be a catechist.*
2. *What does holy water mean in your life?*
3. *As a person blessed and chosen by God, what are the challenges that you face?*

RITUAL ACTION
Gather around the water and pray the following, which is found on p. 41 of the student textbook:

All: **Lord God Almighty,
hear the prayers of your people.
We celebrate your love that created us and saves us.
You made the water of Baptism holy.
By it you give us a new birth in your grace.
You give us new life.
May this water remind us of our Baptism.
We ask this through Christ our Lord. Amen.**
Invite each child forward and sign each with the water.

water

LORD'S PRAYER
Leader: Let us join in the words that Christ has given us.

All: **Our Father . . . for the kingdom, the power, and the glory are yours, now and for ever. Amen.**

CONCLUDING RITE
"Final Blessing," CD/CS–#19, mb–#25, or:

Leader: The Lord be with you.
All: **And also with you.**
Leader: May almighty God bless us, the Father, the Son, ✠ and the Holy Spirit.
All: **Amen!**
Leader: Our celebration has ended. Let us go forth to love and serve our God.
All: **Thanks be to God.**

Concluding Song
Refrain of "Blest Are You, O God" (Canticle of Zachary), CD/CS–#7, mb–#7

Jesus Shares Himself with Us

UNIT 3
CHAPTERS 9–12

Getting Started

Celebrate this ritual during the Advent Season. You may use the "Blessing of the Advent Wreath" found on the CD and cassette or do the simplified version here. It is best to use the parish Advent wreath. If you are unable to do so, use a wreath from home with candles. Placing candles in 6 oz. glasses prevents the flame from being a danger to children.

INTRODUCTORY RITES

Opening Song

"Advent Gathering: Make Ready the Way/Come, O Lord," CD/CS–#3, mb–#3

Use the complete rite as on the CD and cassette or use just the music and proclaim the following:

Leader:	In the name of the Father, and of the Son, and of the Holy Spirit.
All:	**Amen!**
Leader:	The Lord be with you.
All:	**And also with you.**

Opening Comments

Leader: As we gather this Advent Season, we wait and remember how the world once waited for Jesus. We gather around the fire of this Advent wreath. We have lit *(number)* candle(s) for the week(s) we have waited.

Opening Prayer

Leader: Let us pray. *(orans gesture)*
Lord God,
let your blessing come upon us
as we light the candles of this wreath.
May the wreath and its light
be a sign of Christ's promise
to bring us salvation.
May Christ come quickly and not delay.
We ask this through Christ our Lord. Amen!

SCRIPTURE READING

2 Corinthians 1:2–4

A Bible should be on the prayer table. Reverence the Bible and then lift and read directly from it.

Leader: A reading from the Second Letter of Paul to the Corinthians.

I pray that God our Father and the Lord Jesus Christ will be kind to you and will bless you with peace! Praise God, the Father of our Lord Jesus Christ! The Father is a merciful God, who always gives us comfort. He comforts us when we are in trouble, so that we can share that same comfort with others in trouble.

Leader: The word of the Lord.
All: **Thanks be to God.**

Reflection

Share with the group your feelings about the Scripture reading. Use these questions for your personal reflection.

1. *What does the Advent Season mean to you?*
2. *When have you waited for the love and comfort of God?*
3. *Where do you see the comfort of God being shared in the world?*

LORD'S PRAYER

Leader: Let us join in the words that Christ has given us.

All: **Our Father . . . for the kingdom, the power, and the glory are yours, now and for ever. Amen.**

CONCLUDING RITE

"Final Blessing," CD/CS–#19, mb–#25, or:

Leader: The Lord be with you.
All: **And also with you.**
Leader: May almighty God bless us, the Father, the Son, ✠ and the Holy Spirit.
All: **Amen!**
Leader: Our celebration has ended. Let us go forth to love and serve our God.
All: **Thanks be to God.**

Concluding Song

"Prayer for Peace," CD/CS–#13, mb–#16

Jesus Lives in the Church

UNIT 4
CHAPTERS 13–16

Getting Started

In this prayer service we focus on Jesus serving the needs of others and on the use of the general intercessions. If you want to have a sung response, you might use the general intercessions in the music collection. If not, use the intercessions provided here. There will also be time for spontaneous prayer. Prior to the ritual, take time to ask the children about the world they live in and what they feel the group should pray for.

INTRODUCTORY
RITES

Opening Song

"Prayer for Peace," CD/CS–#13, mb–#16

Leader:	In the name of the Father, and of the Son, and of the Holy Spirit.
All:	**Amen!**
Leader:	The Lord be with you.
All:	**And also with you.**

Opening Comments

Leader: As we gather in this Christmas Season, we remember how Jesus came so that all could share in his love. Let us remember those in need.

Opening Prayer

Leader: Let us pray. *(orans gesture)*
Lord Jesus,
in the peace of the Christmas Season,
our hearts are happy.
With animals and angels,
with shepherds and stars,
with Mary and Joseph we sing God's praise.
Through your birth may all people find peace.
We ask this through Christ our Lord. Amen!

SCRIPTURE
READING

Colossians 3:16

A Bible should be on the prayer table. Reverence the Bible and then lift and read directly from it.

Leader: A reading from the Letter of Paul to the Colossians.

Let the message about Christ completely fill your lives, while you use all your wisdom to teach and instruct each other. With thankful hearts, sing psalms, hymns, and spiritual songs to God.

Leader:	The word of the Lord.
All:	**Thanks be to God.**

Reflection

Share with the group your feelings about the Scripture reading. Use these questions for your personal reflection.

1. *What is the message of Christmas that lives in your heart?*
2. *How has God given you wisdom, and how do you use it?*
3. *What situation in the world do you think needs specific prayers?*

INTERCESSIONS   "General Intercessions," in music collection or:

Leader: Jesus came to show us how to care for others. Let us come before God as we pray for those in our world.

Reader: We pray for the people of the Church. Let us pray to the Lord.
All: **Lord, hear our prayer.**

Reader: We pray that you will guide the rulers of nations.
Let us pray to the Lord.

We pray that you will protect unborn children, help people who are poor, and care for people who are elderly. Let us pray to the Lord.

We add our thoughts on what we should pray for.

Insert your own intentions here.

We pray for those who are sick. Let us pray to the Lord.

We pray for those who have died. Let us pray to the Lord.

LORD'S PRAYER
Leader: Let us join in the words that Christ has given us.

All: **Our Father . . . for the kingdom, the power, and the glory are yours, now and for ever. Amen.**

CONCLUDING RITE   "Final Blessing," CD/CS–#19, mb–#25, or:

Leader: The Lord be with you.
All: **And also with you.**
Leader: May almighty God bless us, the Father, the Son, ✠ and the Holy Spirit.
All: **Amen!**
Leader: Our celebration has ended. Let us go forth to love and serve our God.
All: **Thanks be to God.**

Concluding Song
"Walking by Faith," CD/CS–#1, mb–#1

The Sacrament of Reconciliation

UNIT 5
CHAPTERS 17–20

Getting Started

During this ritual we will use an examination of conscience. It is taken from the school- or parish-wide Reconciliation service. When it comes time to kneel and pray, it is suggested that the children pray the Confiteor from Mass. If the students do not know this prayer, use "Lord have mercy, Christ have mercy, Lord have mercy."

INTRODUCTORY RITES

Opening Song

"Blest Are They," CD/CS–#17, mb–#22

Leader: In the name of the Father, and of the Son, and of the Holy Spirit.
All: **Amen!**
Leader: The Lord be with you.
All: **And also with you.**

Opening Comments

Leader: As we gather during this Season of Lent, we admit we have not always done as God has wanted. We ask God to forgive us for we are truly sorry. We know that Jesus will heal us.

Opening Prayer

Leader: Let us pray. *(orans gesture)*
God our Father,
you sent Jesus to be the friend of children.
He came to show us how we can love you, Father,
by loving one another.
He came to take away sin,
which keeps us from being friends,
and hate, which makes us all unhappy.
He promised to send the Holy Spirit to be with us always
so that we can live as your children.
God the Father, Son, and Holy Spirit, be with us always
and help us choose what is right!
We ask this through Christ our Lord. Amen!

SCRIPTURE READING

Luke 7:47–48, 50

A Bible should be on the prayer table. Reverence the Bible and then lift and read directly from it.

Leader: The Lord be with you.
All: **And also with you.**
Leader: A reading from the holy Gospel according to Luke.
All: **Glory to you, O Lord.**

Teacher's note: You may need to explain this Scripture prior to reading it. Set up the story that this is a woman who is truly sorry for her sins and comes to where Jesus is dining to ask forgiveness; then read the Scripture from the Bible.

"So I tell you that all her sins are forgiven, and that is why she has shown great love. But anyone who has been forgiven for only a little will show only a little love." Then Jesus said to the woman, "Your sins are forgiven." But Jesus told the woman, "Because of your faith, you are now saved. May God give you peace!"

Leader: The gospel of the Lord.
All: **Praise to you, Lord Jesus Christ.**

Reflection
Share with the group your feelings about the Scripture reading. Use these questions for your personal reflection.
  1. *Describe a time in your life when you have truly felt forgiven by the love of Jesus.*
  2. *Do you believe Jesus will forgive anything you do for which you are sorry?*
  3. *Describe having to forgive someone else. What was that like?*
  4. *What challenges you in forgiving others?*

RITUAL ACTION

Go into the "Examination of Conscience: Jesus, Heal Us," CD/CS–#16, mb–#20, and end that section with a recitation of an act of contrition, or the Confiteor, or use this alternate text for an examination of conscience:

Leader: As we look at our own lives, let us ask God to forgive us. Please respond, "Heal us and hear us, O God."

Reader: O God, sometimes we have not behaved as your children should.
We come to you and pray . . . *Response.*

O God, we have given trouble to our family members and teachers.
We come to you and pray . . . *Response.*

O God, we have quarreled and called each other names. We come to you and pray . . . *Response.*

O God, we have been lazy at home and in school, and have not been helpful to our families. We come to you and pray . . . *Response.*

O God, we have thought too much of ourselves and have told lies.
We come to you and pray . . . *Response.*

O God, we have not done good to others when we had the chance. We come to you and pray . . . *Response.*

Leader: As children of God who are truly sorry, let us kneel and ask for God's forgiveness.

Leader: Lord, have mercy.
All: **Lord, have mercy.**

Leader: Christ, have mercy.
All: **Christ, have mercy.**

Leader: Lord, have mercy.
All: **Lord, have mercy.**

LORD'S PRAYER

Leader: Let us stand and join in the words that Christ has given us.

All: **Our Father . . . for the kingdom, the power, and the glory are yours, now and for ever. Amen.**

Leader: As children loved by God, let us offer each other a sign of God's peace. *All will offer each other a sign of peace.*

CONCLUDING RITE

"Final Blessing," CD/CS–#19, mb–#25, or:

Leader: The Lord be with you.
All: **And also with you.**
Leader: May almighty God bless us, the Father, the Son, ✠ and the Holy Spirit.
All: **Amen!**
Leader: Our celebration has ended. Let us go forth to love and serve our God.
All: **Thanks be to God.**

Concluding Song
"Deep Down I Know," CD/CS–#10, mb–#12

Jesus Gives Us Sacraments

Getting Started

In this ritual we will venerate a cross. It should be a large cross that all the children will recognize. Perhaps it could be the parish processional cross or one they see each time they gather for a catechetical session. Prior to the service you may want to review an appropriate gesture for venerating a cross. Check the local custom. It is proper to use a simple yet profound bow. In some parishes the people come up and kiss the cross. By doing this ritual in the catechetical session, we are preparing our children to take part in the larger community's celebration of Good Friday.

INTRODUCTORY
RITES

Opening Song

"Song of the Body of Christ," CD/CS–#18, mb–#24

Leader: In the name of the Father, and of the Son, and of the Holy Spirit.
All: **Amen!**
Leader: The Lord be with you.
All: **And also with you.**

Opening Comments

Leader: The Church throughout the world celebrates this holy time of the year with special services. We call this week Holy Week. On Holy Thursday we hear how Jesus loved his friends so much that he sat down and had a final meal with them. During the meal he gave them the gift of the Eucharist—holy bread and wine that are his Body and Blood. On Good Friday we remember how Jesus died on the cross to save us. On Holy Saturday we remember that God the Father raised Jesus from the dead. His resurrection reminds us that we are all welcome to share in the joy of new life. Today let us focus on Jesus' death on the cross and his rising to new life.

Opening Prayer

Leader: Let us pray. *(orans gesture)*
O God our Father,
you gave us Jesus who always obeyed you,
and so you gave him the highest name above all others.
Jesus showed us how to love others.
May we, in turn, be kind and do things that are pleasing to you.
We ask this through Christ our Lord. Amen!

SCRIPTURE
READING

Philippians 2:8–11

A Bible should be on the prayer table. Reverence the Bible and then lift and read directly from it.

Leader: A reading from the Letter of Paul to the Philippians.

Christ was humble. He obeyed God and even died on a cross. Then God gave Christ the highest place and honored his name above all others. So at the name of Jesus everyone will bow down, those in heaven, on earth, and under the earth. And to the glory of God the Father everyone will openly agree, "Jesus Christ is Lord!"

Leader: The word of the Lord.
All: **Thanks be to God.**

Reflection
Share with the group your feelings about the Scripture reading. Use these questions for your personal reflection.
1. *When you look at the cross of Jesus, what does it mean to you?*
2. *What are the crosses in your life?*
3. *What does the term "glory of the cross" mean to you?*
4. *How does Good Friday differ from Holy Saturday, and how are they reflected in the sadness and joy of your own life?*

RITUAL ACTION

For veneration of cross, see notes from "Getting Started."

Leader: We are now going to reverence the cross. As Christians we know that after Jesus died on the cross, God the Father raised him to new life. Let us honor the cross by very reverently bowing *(or whatever the tradition is)* before the cross.
Older students might hold the cross and candles on either side of the cross. After the veneration, you may want to sing the refrain of "Song of the Body of Christ."

LORD'S PRAYER

Leader: Let us join in the words that Christ has given us.

All: **Our Father . . . for the kingdom, the power, and the glory are yours, now and for ever. Amen.**

CONCLUDING RITE

"Final Blessing," CD/CS–#19, mb–#25, or:

Leader: The Lord be with you.
All: **And also with you.**
Leader: May almighty God bless us, the Father, the Son, ✠ and the Holy Spirit.
All: **Amen!**
Leader: Our celebration has ended. Let us go forth to love and serve our God.
All: **Thanks be to God.**

Concluding Song
"Prayer for Peace," CD/CS–#13, mb–#16

Jesus, Lord of All Creation

UNIT 7
CHAPTERS 25–28

Getting Started

As the catechetical year comes to an end, take time to review where you have been this year. Review highlights of each of the seven prayer rituals. This ritual works well when done around the Easter baptismal font. If possible, gather around the parish font. If not, bring holy water from church and pour it into a large bowl, light a candle, and gather.

INTRODUCTORY RITES

Opening Song

"This Is the Day" (Psalm 118), CD/CS–#12, mb–#14

Leader: In the name of the Father, and of the Son, and of the Holy Spirit.
All: **Amen!**
Leader: The Lord be with you.
All: **And also with you.**

Opening Comments

Leader: On Holy Saturday the priest *(give name, if possible)* blessed this water. It is holy water, and today we celebrate with it. In Baptism we were baptized into the family of Christ.

Opening Prayer

Leader: Let us pray. *(orans gesture)*
God our Father, Creator of all,
we celebrate with Easter joy.
The Lord appeared to those who had begun to lose hope.
May the risen Lord breathe on our minds.
May he open our eyes that we may know him in the breaking of bread.
May we follow him in his risen life.
We ask this through Christ our Lord. Amen!

SCRIPTURE READING

Mark 16:15–17a, 18b

A Bible should be on the prayer table. Reverence the Bible and then lift and read directly from it.

Leader: The Lord be with you.
All: **And also with you.**
Leader: A reading from the holy Gospel according to Mark.
All: **Glory to you, O Lord.**

Jesus told his disciples: Go and preach the good news to everyone in the world. Anyone who believes me and is baptized will be saved. But anyone who refuses to believe me will be condemned. Everyone who believes me will be able to do wonderful things. They will also heal sick people by placing their hands on them.

Leader: The gospel of the Lord.

All: **Praise to you, Lord Jesus Christ.**

Reflection

Share with the group your feelings about the Scripture reading. Use these questions for your personal reflection.

1. *What is the "good news" to tell others?*
2. *What events occurred this past year that hold some importance for you?*
3. *What have you learned this year that you will take out into the world?*

RITUAL ACTION

Use "Greeting and Thanksgiving Over Water Already Blessed" found in "People of God/Alleluia," CD/CS–#8, mb–#8, or the following:

Leader: God our Father, you give us grace through special signs, which tell us of the wonders of your power. Please respond, "Blessed are you, O Lord our God!"

Move your hand through the water during the invocations. You may also want to have the students move their hands through the water during their response.

At the dawn of creation, your Spirit breathed on the waters. *Response.*

You made the waters of the great flood a sign of the end of sin. *Response.*

Through the waters of the Red Sea, you led Israel out of slavery. *Response.*

In the waters of the Jordan, your Son was baptized by John and sealed by the Spirit. *Response.*

Water and blood flowed from Jesus' side as he hung on the cross. *Response.*

In the Sacrament of Baptism, may all those you have created in your likeness be cleansed from sin and rise to new birth by water and the Holy Spirit. Amen.

I invite everyone to come forward and sign themselves with these waters.

The leader blesses him/herself making the Sign of the Cross with the holy water and then the students do the same.

LORD'S PRAYER

Leader: Let us join in the words that Christ has given us.

All: **Our Father . . . for the kingdom, the power, and the glory are yours, now and for ever. Amen.**

CONCLUDING RITE "Final Blessing," CD/CS–#19, mb–#25, or:

Leader: The Lord be with you.
All: **And also with you.**
Leader: May almighty God bless us, the Father, the Son, ✠ and the Holy Spirit.
All: **Amen!**
Leader: Our celebration has ended. Let us go forth to love and serve our God.
All: **Thanks be to God.**

Concluding Song
"Walking by Faith," CD/CS–#1, mb–#1

Created for Community

Getting Started

During this year of services we will be focusing on different parts of the Eucharistic celebration. There are certain rites that can be celebrated that will enhance the students' participation in the Eucharistic liturgy. The writer hopes that through the praying of these services, the students will celebrate more fully in the Eucharistic worship of the community. Look carefully at the ritual action and decide how you can best facilitate the movement of the children.

INTRODUCTORY RITES

Opening Song

"Walking by Faith," CD/CS–#1, mb–#1

Leader: In the name of the Father, and of the Son, and of the Holy Spirit.
All: **Amen!**
Leader: The Lord be with you.
All: **And also with you.**

Opening Comments

Leader: As we gather this year, let us focus on how God welcomes us to share in the gift of his creation. All that is around us is a gift from God. Let us care for all things as special gifts from God.

Opening Prayer

Leader: Let us pray. *(orans gesture)*
Praise to you, O Lord our God,
for all your creatures!
For Brother Sun and our Sister Moon, we praise you!
For our Brother Wind and our Sister Water, we praise you!
For our Brother Fire and our Mother Earth, we praise you!
May our actions this year always celebrate the gifts of this earth.
We praise you through Christ our Lord. Amen!

SCRIPTURE READING

Matthew 5:14–16

A Bible should be on the prayer table. Reverence the Bible and then lift and read directly from it.

Leader: The Lord be with you.
All: **And also with you.**
Leader: A reading from the holy Gospel according to Matthew.
All: **Glory to you, O Lord.**

You are like light for the whole world. A city built on top of a hill cannot be hidden, and no one would light a lamp and put it under a clay pot. A lamp is placed on a lampstand, where it can give light to everyone in the house. Make your light shine, so that others will see the good that you do and will praise your Father in heaven.

Leader: The gospel of the Lord.
All: **Praise to you, Lord Jesus Christ.**

Reflection
Share with the group your feelings about the Scripture reading. Use these questions for your personal reflection.
  1. *When have you been like a light for the world?*
  2. *Sharing faith is a way of lighting the path for others. Who has been a light of God in your life?*
  3. *What challenges you in keeping your light shining for all?*

Song
"Blest Are You, O God" (Canticle of Zachary), CD/CS–#7, mb–#7

RITUAL ACTION *Invite each child forward and bless them, saying, "N., you are a child of God, a child of his creation. May God be with you this year as you walk by faith. Amen."*

blessing

LORD'S PRAYER
Leader: Let us join in the words that Christ has given us.

All: **Our Father . . . for the kingdom, the power, and the glory are yours, now and for ever. Amen.**

CONCLUDING RITE "Final Blessing," CD/CS–#19, mb–#25, or:

Leader: The Lord be with you.
All: **And also with you.**
Leader: May almighty God bless us, the Father, the Son, ✠ and the Holy Spirit.
All: **Amen!**
Leader: Our celebration has ended. Let us go forth to love and serve our God.
All: **Thanks be to God.**

Concluding Song
"Alleluia/Gospel Acclamation," CD/CS–#5, mb–#5

People of God

Getting Started

During this service we celebrate a penitential rite. Look at the Sacramentary for other options for this rite.

INTRODUCTORY
RITES

Opening Song

"God's People" (Psalm 100), CD/CS–#2, mb–#2

Leader: In the name of the Father, and of the Son, and of the Holy Spirit.
All: **Amen!**
Leader: The Lord be with you.
All: **And also with you.**

Opening Comments

Leader: As people of God we need to recognize that God is greater than all of us. The saints knew this and always praised God for helping them in times of trouble. Let us turn to God to ask for his love and praise his mercy.

Penitential Rite

Lord Jesus, you are light for a world that sometimes lives in darkness. Lord, have mercy.
All: **Lord, have mercy.**

Leader: Christ Jesus, you lift us from times of sadness. Christ, have mercy.
All: **Christ, have mercy.**

Leader: Lord Jesus, when we do wrong, you show us the ways of faith and love. Lord, have mercy.
All: **Lord, have mercy.**

Leader: May almighty God have mercy on us, forgive us our sins, and bring us to everlasting life.
All: **Amen.**

Opening Prayer

Leader: Let us pray. *(orans gesture)*
All powerful and ever-living God,
we rejoice in holy men and women of every time and place.
May their prayers bring us your forgiveness and love.
We ask this through Christ our Lord. Amen!

SCRIPTURE
READING

2 Corinthians 13:13

A Bible should be on the prayer table. Reverence the Bible and then lift and read directly from it.

Leader: A reading from the Second Letter of Paul to the Corinthians.

I pray that the Lord Jesus Christ will bless you and be kind to you! May God bless you with his love, and may the Holy Spirit join all your hearts together.

Leader: The word of the Lord.
All: **Thanks be to God.**

Reflection

Share with the group your feelings about the Scripture reading. Use these questions for your personal reflection.

1. *How have you felt the blessing of God's love in your life?*
2. *When has God's love lifted you from the depths of your wrongdoings?*
3. *Who in your life needs God's blessing, and how can you share that blessing with this person?*

Song

Refrain of "Blest Are You, O God" (Canticle of Zachary), CD/CS–#7, mb–#7

LORD'S PRAYER

Leader: Let us join in the words that Christ has given us.

All: **Our Father . . . for the kingdom, the power, and the glory are yours, now and for ever. Amen.**

CONCLUDING RITE

"Final Blessing," CD/CS–#19, mb–#25, or:

Leader: The Lord be with you.
All: **And also with you.**
Leader: May almighty God bless us, the Father, the Son, ✠ and the Holy Spirit.
All: **Amen!**
Leader: Our celebration has ended. Let us go forth to love and serve our God.
All: **Thanks be to God.**

Concluding Song

"Walking by Faith," CD/CS–#1, mb–#1

The Body of Christ

Getting Started

During this service we focus on God's word and our call to serve our brothers and sisters. We can do this by praying for them and their needs. Focus on having the children share their thoughts and intercessions. Take time during the general intercessions to ask them what they feel the group should pray for.

INTRODUCTORY
RITES

Opening Song

"Advent Gathering: Make Ready the Way," CD/CS–#3, mb–#3
Use "Make Ready the Way" only for the gathering. "Come, O Lord" will be used for the general intercessions.

Leader:	In the name of the Father, and of the Son, and of the Holy Spirit.
All:	**Amen!**
Leader:	The Lord be with you.
All:	**And also with you.**

Opening Comments

Leader: During this Season of Advent, we remember how Jesus came to serve all people. Let us take time to remember how we all must be like Jesus and care for everyone, even those who are poor and who need our prayers.

Opening Prayer

Leader: Let us pray. *(orans gesture)*
Dear God,
we are part of your family.
As we look forward to celebrating the birthday of your Son, Jesus,
we remember Noah's family, Abraham and Sarah,
Jacob, Joseph, Moses and Joshua, Ruth and David.
These are people who never lost faith in your promise.
In love and faith, may we always serve our brothers and sisters in need.
We ask this through Christ our Lord. Amen!

SCRIPTURE
READING

Luke 4:16–21

A Bible should be on the prayer table. Reverence the Bible and then lift and read directly from it.

Leader:	The Lord be with you.
All:	**And also with you.**
Leader:	A reading from the holy Gospel according to Luke.
All:	**Glory to you, O Lord.**

Jesus went back to Nazareth, where he had been brought up, and as usual he went to the meeting place on the Sabbath. When he stood up to read from the Scriptures, he was given the book of Isaiah the prophet. He opened it and read, "The Lord's Spirit has come to me, because he has chosen me to tell the good news to the poor. The Lord has sent me to announce freedom for prisoners, to give sight to the blind, to free everyone who suffers, and to say, 'This is the year the Lord has chosen.'" Jesus closed the book, then handed it back to the man in charge and sat down. Everyone in the meeting place looked straight at Jesus. Then Jesus said to them, "What you have just heard me read has come true today."

Leader: The gospel of the Lord.

All: **Praise to you, Lord Jesus Christ.**

Reflection

Share with the group your feelings about the Scripture reading. Use these questions for your personal reflection.

1. *What message does Jesus bring to people who are poor?*
2. *How have you seen this message in your own life?*
3. *To whom in this world can you bring this message of hope?*

Song

"Holy Is Your Name" (Canticle of Mary), CD/CS–#4, mb–#4

If this song seems too long for the children, you could just teach the refrain and associate this with the words of the Blessed Mother.

INTERCESSIONS   *For a response, use the refrain from "Come, O Lord" from CD/CS–#3, mb–#3.*

Leader: Let us come before God with our needs.

Reader: For all who bring the light of God by sharing faith. Let us pray to the Lord. *Response.*

For all who seek peace throughout the world. Let us pray to the Lord. *Response.*

For those whose lives are lonely and filled with pain. Let us pray to the Lord. *Response.*

Insert your own intentions here.

For those who are ill and hope for the healing touch of God. Let us pray to the Lord. *Response.*

For those who have died and now live with Jesus in heaven. Let us pray to the Lord. *Response.*

LORD'S PRAYER

Leader:　Let us join in the words that Christ has given us.

All:　**Our Father . . . for the kingdom, the power, and the glory are yours, now and for ever. Amen.**

CONCLUDING RITE

"Final Blessing," CD/CS–#19, mb–#25, or:

Leader:　The Lord be with you.
All:　**And also with you.**
Leader:　May almighty God bless us, the Father, the Son, ✠ and the Holy Spirit.
All:　**Amen!**
Leader:　Our celebration has ended. Let us go forth to love and serve our God.
All:　**Thanks be to God.**

Concluding Song
"Prayer for Peace," CD/CS–#13, mb–#16

Guided by the Holy Spirit

UNIT 4
CHAPTERS 13–16

Getting Started
During this service we focus on the creed. The ritual action on the creed may be done in a question and answer format or by using the Apostles' Creed. If your parish is celebrating Baptisms during these weeks, consider attending one and discuss how this ritual reflects the creed.

INTRODUCTORY RITES

Opening Song
"Alleluia/Gospel Acclamation," CD/CS–#5, mb–#5

Leader: In the name of the Father, and of the Son, and of the Holy Spirit.
All: **Amen!**
Leader: The Lord be with you.
All: **And also with you.**

Opening Comments
Leader: As children of faith and love, we gather to celebrate all that we believe. Let us focus on the love God has given us by letting us be called children of God.

Opening Prayer
Leader: Let us pray. *(orans gesture)*
God of Mary and Joseph, of shepherds and animals,
your love has gifted this world with your Son, Jesus.
Fill our hearts with welcoming joy,
gentleness, and thanksgiving,
and guide our steps in the way of peace.
We ask this through Christ our Lord. Amen!

SCRIPTURE READING

Romans 12:3–5, 7–8
A Bible should be on the prayer table. Reverence the Bible and then lift and read directly from it.
Leader: A reading from the Letter of Paul to the Romans.

I realize how kind God has been to me, and so I tell each of you not to think you are better than you really are. Use good sense and measure yourself by the amount of faith that God has given you. A body is made up of many parts, and each of them has its own use. That's how it is with us. There are many of us, but we each are part of the body of Christ, as well as part of one another. If we can serve others, we should serve. If we can teach, we should teach. If we can encourage others, we should encourage them. If we can give, we should be generous. If we are leaders, we should do our best. If we are good to others, we should do it cheerfully.

Leader: The word of the Lord.
All: **Thanks be to God.**

Reflection

Share with the group your feelings about the Scripture reading. Use these questions for your personal reflection.

1. What gift do you bring to the Body of Christ, the Church?
2. Who has served you well in your life?
3. Who in this world inspires you to serve others?

Song

"Holy Is Your Name" (Canticle of Mary), CD/CS–#4, mb–#4

RITUAL ACTION   *Recite the Apostles' Creed found on page 176 of the student text or use the following:*

Leader: Do you believe in God, the Father almighty, creator of heaven and earth?

All: **I do.**

Leader: Do you believe in Jesus Christ, his only Son, our Lord, who was born of the Virgin Mary, was crucified, died, and was buried, rose from the dead, and is now seated at the right hand of the Father?

All: **I do.**

Leader: Do you believe in the Holy Spirit, the holy catholic Church, the communion of saints, the forgiveness of sins, the resurrection of the body, and life everlasting?

All: **I do.**

Leader: All powerful and ever-living God, keep us faithful to our Lord Jesus Christ, for ever and ever. Amen.

CONCLUDING RITE   "Final Blessing," CD/CS–#19, mb–#25, or:

Leader: The Lord be with you.
All: **And also with you.**
Leader: May almighty God bless us, the Father, the Son, ✠ and the Holy Spirit.
All: **Amen!**
Leader: Our celebration has ended. Let us go forth to love and serve our God.
All: **Thanks be to God.**

Concluding Song

"Walking by Faith," CD/CS–#1, mb–#1

Temple of the Holy Spirit

UNIT 5
CHAPTERS 17–20

Getting Started

During this service we focus on the rite of the Lord's Prayer and the sharing of the sign of peace with one another. During Lent we are asked to pray, fast, and give alms. As a ritual action following the sign of peace, consider ritually collecting items for a charity your parish is involved with—a soup kitchen, hospice, or mission.

INTRODUCTORY
RITES

Opening Song

"Blest Are They," CD/CS–#17, mb–#22

Leader: In the name of the Father, and of the Son, and of the Holy Spirit.
All: **Amen!**
Leader: The Lord be with you.
All: **And also with you.**

Opening Comments

Leader: During this holy Season of Lent, we remember to pray, fast, and give to people who are in need. Let us take time to reflect on God's love for each of us.

Opening Prayer

Leader: Let us pray. *(orans gesture)*
Thank you, O Lord Jesus Christ,
for all that you have given us.
Most merciful Redeemer, Friend, and Brother,
may we know you more clearly,
love you more dearly,
and follow you more nearly.
We ask this through Christ our Lord. Amen!

SCRIPTURE
READING

Matthew 5:1–12

A Bible should be on the prayer table. Reverence the Bible and then lift and read directly from it.

Leader: The Lord be with you.
All: **And also with you.**
Leader: A reading from the holy Gospel according to Matthew.
All: **Glory to you, O Lord.**

When Jesus saw the crowds, he went up on the side of a mountain and sat down. Jesus' disciples gathered around him, and he taught them: God blesses those people who depend only on him. They belong to the kingdom of heaven! God blesses those people who grieve. They will find comfort! God blesses those people who are humble. The earth will belong to them! God blesses those people who want to obey him more than to eat or drink. They will be given what they want! God blesses those people who are merciful. They will be treated with mercy! God blesses those people whose

hearts are pure. They will see him! God blesses those people who make peace. They will be called his children! God blesses those people who are treated badly for doing right. They belong to the kingdom of heaven. God will bless you when people insult you, mistreat you, and tell all kinds of evil lies about you because of me. Be happy and excited! You will have a great reward in heaven. People did these same things to the prophets who lived long ago.

Leader: The gospel of the Lord.
All: **Praise to you, Lord Jesus Christ.**

Reflection
Share with the group your feelings about the Scripture reading. Use these questions for your personal reflection.
1. *Which of the Beatitudes are of special interest to you?*
2. *When have you lived one of the Beatitudes?*
3. *Which Beatitude challenges you?*

Song
"Lord, Be with Me" (Psalm 91), CD/CS–#14, mb–#17

INTERCESSIONS "General Intercessions," in music collection or:

Leader: Let us come before God with our needs.

Reader: For those of the Church who lead us in faith. Let us pray to the Lord.
All: **Lord, hear our prayer.**

Reader: For those who work for peace in the world. Let us pray to the Lord.

For those who are homeless and feel as though no one loves them. Let us pray to the Lord.

Insert your own intentions here.

For those who are ill. Let us pray to the Lord.

For those who have died. Let us pray to the Lord.

LORD'S PRAYER
Leader: Let us join in the words that Christ has given us.

All: **Our Father . . . for the kingdom, the power, and the glory are yours, now and for ever. Amen.**

Sign of Peace

Leader: Lord Jesus Christ, you said to your apostles: I leave you peace, my peace I give you. Look not on our sins, but on the faith of your Church, and grant us the peace and unity of your kingdom where you live for ever and ever.

All: **Amen.**

Leader: The peace of the Lord be with you always.
All: **And also with you.**
Leader: Let us offer each other a sign of peace.

CONCLUDING RITE   "Final Blessing," CD/CS–#19, mb–#25, or:

Leader: The Lord be with you.
All: **And also with you.**
Leader: May almighty God bless us, the Father, the Son, ✠ and the Holy Spirit.
All: **Amen!**
Leader: Our celebration has ended. Let us go forth to love and serve our God.
All: **Thanks be to God.**

Concluding Song
"Deep Down I Know," CD/CS–#10, mb–#12

Belonging, Healing, Serving

UNIT 6
CHAPTERS 21–24

Getting Started

During this ritual we reflect on Holy Week and on the apostles' response to God's call. We do this by carrying out a washing of the feet in the classroom. Although this ritual is done on Holy Thursday, the action may have more meaning for children this age if first done in a catechetical setting. To do this you need warm water with some lemon extract added to it. Have a few basins and a few pitchers. You will also need many towels. Have the children bring one from home to donate to the parish or ask the parish sacristan if there is a large quantity used at Holy Thursday which you could borrow. Select some students to pour the water over the feet. You may wish to invite other adults to help you–the principal, DRE, or the students' family members. Yes, the first time you do this it will seem strange and the students may laugh, but that is OK. If the leaders are reverent, the rite will have a powerful effect on the students during Holy Thursday. You will need to reflect on this rite afterwards. Be sure to answer how you felt during the experience.

INTRODUCTORY RITES

Opening Song

"Song of the Body of Christ," CD/CS–#18, mb–#24

Leader:	In the name of the Father, and of the Son, and of the Holy Spirit.
All:	**Amen!**
Leader:	The Lord be with you.
All:	**And also with you.**

Opening Comments

Leader: As the Church, we celebrate this very special season. We remember how Jesus suffered, died, and rose for each of us. We also remember how Jesus came to serve each and every one of us.

Opening Prayer

Leader: Let us pray. *(orans gesture)*
Loving God,
you take every family under your care
and know our physical and spiritual needs.
Strengthen us with your grace
so that we may grow in faith and love.
We ask this through Christ our Lord. Amen!

SCRIPTURE READING

John 13:4–8

A Bible should be on the prayer table. Reverence the Bible and then lift and read directly from it.

Leader:	The Lord be with you.
All:	**And also with you.**
Leader:	A reading from the holy Gospel according to John.
All:	**Glory to you, O Lord.**

During a meal Jesus got up, removed his outer garment, and wrapped a towel around his waist. He put some water into a large bowl. Then he began washing his disciples' feet and drying them with the towel he was wearing. But when he came to Simon Peter, that disciple asked, "Lord, are you going to wash my feet?" Jesus answered, "You don't really know what I am doing, but later you will understand." "You will never wash my feet!" Peter replied. "If I don't wash you," Jesus told him, "you don't really belong to me."

Leader: The gospel of the Lord.
All: **Praise to you, Lord Jesus Christ.**

Reflection

Share with the group your feelings about the Scripture reading. Use these questions for your personal reflection.

1. *What would it have been like to have your feet washed by Jesus?*
2. *What does it mean for you to wash feet? Why would you wash someone's feet?*
3. *Whose feet are you asked to wash?*
4. *Who has washed feet in this world? Reflect on the life of Mother Teresa.*

Song

"Like the Sweet Fragrance" (Canticle of Sirach), CD/CS–#11, mb–#13

RITUAL ACTION

Leader: We are now going to do as the Scripture said. As a class we will wash feet. It may seem strange, but remember Christ's call to his apostles. *During this time you may need many adults to help you, and you may need to combine a few classes together to save time. See specific instructions above. Also inquire into how the parish washes feet on Holy Thursday. Use this procedure as your model.*

INTERCESSIONS

"General Intercessions," in music collection or:

Leader: Let us pray to God for those who serve us.

Reader: For priests who lead us to God. Let us pray to the Lord.
All: **Lord, hear our prayer.**

Reader: For priests who forgive us in God's name. Let us pray to the Lord.

For married people who lead one another to God. Let us pray to the Lord.

For all people who are willing to say "I'm sorry." Let us pray to the Lord.

LORD'S PRAYER

Leader: Let us join in the words that Christ has given us.

All: **Our Father . . . for the kingdom, the power, and the glory are yours, now and for ever. Amen.**

CONCLUDING RITE

"Final Blessing," CD/CS–#19, mb–#25, or:

Leader: The Lord be with you.
All: **And also with you.**
Leader: May almighty God bless us, the Father, the Son, ✠ and the Holy Spirit.
All: **Amen!**
Leader: Our celebration has ended. Let us go forth to love and serve our God.
All: **Thanks be to God.**

Concluding Song

"Deep Down I Know," CD/CS–#10, mb–#12

Yesterday, Today, and Tomorrow

Getting Started

As the catechetical year comes to an end, take time to review where you have been this year. Review some highlights of each of the seven prayer rituals. This ritual works well when done around the Easter baptismal font. If possible, gather around the parish font. If not, bring holy water from church and pour it into a large bowl, light a candle, and gather.

INTRODUCTORY
RITES

Opening Song

Verses 1 and 2 from "People of God/Alleluia," CD/CS–#8, mb–#8

Leader: In the name of the Father, and of the Son, and of the Holy Spirit.
All: **Amen!**
Leader: The Lord be with you.
All: **And also with you.**

Opening Comments

Leader: As we come to the end of this year, we celebrate with the whole Church that Jesus has risen from the dead. He is alive in the world today. Jesus lives for ever! We are the Church of Christ. Let us celebrate! Alleluia!

Opening Prayer

Leader: Let us pray. (*orans gesture*)
God our Father,
by raising Christ your Son,
you conquered the power of death
and opened for us the way to eternal life.
Let our celebration today
raise us up and renew our lives
by the Spirit that is within us.
We ask this through Christ our Lord. Amen!

SCRIPTURE
READING

Ephesians 1:15–18

A Bible should be on the prayer table. Reverence the Bible and then lift and read directly from it.

Leader: A reading from the Letter to the Ephesians.

I have heard about your faith in the Lord Jesus and your love for all of God's people. So I never stop being grateful for you, as I mention you in my prayers. I ask the glorious Father and God of our Lord Jesus Christ to give you his Spirit. The Spirit will make you wise and let you understand what it means to know God. My prayer is that light will flood your hearts and that you will understand the hope that was given to you when God chose you. Then you will discover the glorious blessings that will be yours together with all of God's people.

Leader: The word of the Lord.
All: **Thanks be to God.**

Reflection

Share with the group your feelings about the Scripture reading. Use these questions for your personal reflection.

1. *As you come to the end of the year, reflect on the things from these sessions for which you are grateful.*
2. *What is your prayer and hope for your students?*
3. *What commitments do you make to the mission of Christ?*

Song

"This Is the Day" (Psalm 118), CD/CS–#12, mb–#14

RITUAL ACTION   **Renewal of Baptismal Promises**

If possible, gather around the parish font or use holy water from the parish. If not, gather in a circle and end the ritual by having each student sign one another.

Leader: Do you reject evil and renew your commitment to Jesus Christ?
All: **I do.**

Leader: Do you believe in God, the Father almighty, Creator of heaven and earth?
All: **I do.**

Leader: Do you believe in Jesus Christ, Son of God?
All: **I do.**

Leader: Do you believe in the Holy Spirit?
All: **I do.**

Leader: Will you proclaim by word and example the good news of God in Christ?
All: **I will, with God's help.**

Leader: Will you strive for justice and peace among all people?
All: **I will, with God's help.**

Leader: *(if water is present)* Let us come to the Easter waters and sign one another.

LORD'S PRAYER

Leader: Let us join in the words that Christ has given us.

All: **Our Father . . . for the kingdom, the power, and the glory are yours, now and for ever. Amen.**

CONCLUDING RITE "Final Blessing," CD/CS–#19, mb–#25, or:

Leader:	The Lord be with you.
All:	**And also with you.**
Leader:	May almighty God bless us, the Father, the Son, ✠ and the Holy Spirit.
All:	**Amen!**
Leader:	Our celebration has ended. Let us go forth to love and serve our God.
All:	**Thanks be to God.**

Concluding Song
"Walking by Faith," CD/CS–#1, mb–#1

Created to Love

Getting Started

As we pray together this year, we will be asked to look at the many choices we make in our lives. These services are a call to listen and to respond to God's word in our decision making. We are responsible for ourselves and the world we live in. We will take time during each celebration to reflect on how our decisions affect ourselves and the world.

Opening Song

"Walking by Faith," CD/CS–#1, mb–#1

Leader:	In the name of the Father, and of the Son, and of the Holy Spirit.
All:	**Amen!**
Leader:	The Lord be with you.
All:	**And also with you.**

Opening Comments

Leader: As we gather this year, let us turn to God and praise him for giving us the earth and for giving us the ability to make choices.

Opening Prayer

Leader: Let us pray. *(orans gesture)*
Lord, our God,
you are great indeed!
How wonderful are your works!
In wisdom you created them all.
The earth is full of your creatures.
When you send forth your breath, they are created,
and you renew the face of the earth.
We will sing to the Lord all the days of our lives.
We ask this through Christ our Lord. Amen!

Luke 10:25–28

A Bible should be on the prayer table. Reverence the Bible and then lift and read directly from it.

Leader:	The Lord be with you.
All:	**And also with you.**
Leader:	A reading from the holy Gospel according to Luke.
All:	**Glory to you, O Lord.**

An expert in the Law of Moses stood up and asked Jesus a question to see what he would say. "Teacher," he asked, "what must I do to have eternal life?" Jesus answered, "What is written in the Scriptures? How do you understand them?" The man replied, "The Scriptures say, 'Love the Lord

your God with all your heart, soul, strength, and mind.' They also say, 'Love your neighbors as much as you love yourself.'" Jesus said, "You have given the right answer. If you do this, you will have eternal life."

Leader: The gospel of the Lord.
All: **Praise to you, Lord Jesus Christ.**

Reflection
Share with the group your feelings about the Scripture reading. Use these questions for your personal reflection.

1. *How do you apply these two commandments to your life?*
2. *How does your ability to fully live one of these commandments affect the other one?*
3. *What challenges you in your life to live these commandments?*

Song
"Blest Are You, O God" (Canticle of Zachary), CD/CS–#7, mb–#7

RITUAL ACTION *Invite the students to come forward and pray with each one, saying, "N., may God be with you as you study the ways of the Lord. Amen."*

blessing prayer

INTERCESSIONS "General Intercessions," in music collection or:

Leader: Let us come before God with our needs.

Reader: For the Church and all who show us the ways of the Lord.
Let us pray to the Lord.
All: **Lord, hear our prayer.**

Reader: For world leaders and all people who choose ways of peace.
Let us pray to the Lord.

Insert your own intentions here.

For those who are sick and are in need of our prayers.
Let us pray to the Lord.

For those who have died. Let us pray to the Lord.

LORD'S PRAYER
Leader: Let us join in the words that Christ has given us.

All: **Our Father . . . for the kingdom, the power, and the glory are yours, now and for ever. Amen.**

CONCLUDING RITE "Final Blessing," CD/CS–#19, mb–#25, or:

Leader:	The Lord be with you.
All:	**And also with you.**
Leader:	May almighty God bless us, the Father, the Son, ✠ and the Holy Spirit.
All:	**Amen!**
Leader:	Our celebration has ended. Let us go forth to love and serve our God.
All:	**Thanks be to God.**

Concluding Song
"Alleluia/Gospel Acclamation," CD/CS–#5, mb–#5

Choosing to Love God

UNIT 2
CHAPTERS 5–8

Getting Started

During this prayer service you are to choose a saint whose life embodied right choices. During the ritual action, chant a Litany of the Saints used by the parish community. A popular litany can be found in GIA's RitualSong hymnal, #977 and the Gather Comprehensive hymnal, #795.

INTRODUCTORY RITES

Opening Song

"Blest Are You, O God" (Canticle of Zachary), CD/CS–#7, mb–#7

Leader: In the name of the Father, and of the Son, and of the Holy Spirit.
All: **Amen!**
Leader: The Lord be with you.
All: **And also with you.**

Opening Comments

Leader: As we go through life we all have to make choices. Men and women we know as saints were also faced with choices. They usually chose ways that were pleasing to God. We must face our God and ask for inspiration as we make choices in our own life.

Opening Prayer

Leader: Let us pray. *(orans gesture)*
All-powerful God and Father of our Lord Jesus Christ,
by water and the Holy Spirit
you freed us from sin
and gave us new life.
Send your Holy Spirit upon us
to be our Helper and Guide.
Give us the spirit of wisdom and understanding,
the spirit of right judgment and courage,
the spirit of knowledge and reverence.
Fill us with the spirit of wonder and awe in your presence.
We ask this through Christ our Lord. Amen!

SCRIPTURE READING

1 John 3:1–2

A Bible should be on the prayer table. Reverence the Bible and then lift and read directly from it.

Leader: A reading from the First Letter of John.

Think how much the Father loves us. He loves us so much that he lets us be called his children, as we truly are. But since the people of this world did not know who Christ is, they don't know who we are. My dear friends, we are already God's children, though what we will be hasn't yet been seen. But we do know that when Christ returns, we will be like him, because we will see him as he truly is.

Leader: The word of the Lord.
All: **Thanks be to God.**

Reflection

Share with the group your feelings about the Scripture reading. Use these questions for your personal reflection.

1. *What does it mean to be called a "child of God"?*
2. *What saint inspires you when you make choices?*
3. *How can the life of a saint inspire you to work for the needs of those who have less than you do?*

Song

"God's People" (Psalm 100), CD/CS–#2, mb–#2

RITUAL ACTION

Leader: Let us now name some of the saints whose lives are important to us as Catholics. We call this a litany, and after each saint's name, we respond, "pray for us."

Chant a Litany of the Saints here.

LORD'S PRAYER

Leader: Let us join in the words that Christ has given us.

All: **Our Father . . . for the kingdom, the power, and the glory are yours, now and for ever. Amen.**

CONCLUDING RITE

"Final Blessing," CD/CS–#19, mb–#25, or:

Leader: The Lord be with you.
All: **And also with you.**
Leader: May almighty God bless us, the Father, the Son, ✠ and the Holy Spirit.
All: **Amen!**
Leader: Our celebration has ended. Let us go forth to love and serve our God.
All: **Thanks be to God.**

Concluding Song

"Walking by Faith," CD/CS–#1, mb–#1

The Way of Jesus

UNIT 3
CHAPTERS 9–12

Getting Started

During this prayer service we will use the examination of conscience used in the school- or parish-wide celebration of reconciliation. Prior to this service you may want to review the Confiteor: (I confess to almighty God . . .).

INTRODUCTORY
RITES

Opening Song

"Prayer for Peace," CD/CS–#13, mb–#16

Leader: In the name of the Father, and of the Son, and of the Holy Spirit.
All: **Amen!**
Leader: The Lord be with you.
All: **And also with you.**

Opening Comments

Leader: As we gather in this Season of Advent, we take time to look at the choices we have made in our lives. As we await the birth of Christ, let us turn our minds toward our love and concern for all humans.

Opening Prayer

Leader: Let us pray. *(orans gesture)*
O God, we love you above all things,
with our whole heart and soul,
because you are all-good and worthy of all love.
We love our neighbor as ourselves for the love of you.
We forgive all who have injured us
and ask pardon on all whom we have injured.
We ask this through Christ our Lord. Amen!

SCRIPTURE
READING

Philippians 4:4–7

A Bible should be on the prayer table. Reverence the Bible and then lift and read directly from it.

Leader: A reading from the Letter of Paul to the Philippians.

Always be glad because of the Lord! I will say it again: Be glad. Always be gentle with others. The Lord will soon be here. Don't worry about anything, but pray about everything. With thankful hearts offer up your prayers and requests to God. Then, because you belong to Christ Jesus, God will bless you with peace that no one can completely understand. And this peace will control the way you think and feel.

Leader: The word of the Lord.
All: **Thanks be to God.**

Reflection

Share with the group your feelings about the Scripture reading. Use these questions for your personal reflection.

1. *When have you let go of your concerns and trusted completely in God?*
2. *What prevents you from always trusting in God?*
3. *What issues in our world need to be left in the hands of God, or at least have God inspire the decisions?*

Song

"Holy Is Your Name" (Canticle of Mary), CD/CS–#4, mb–#4

RITUAL ACTION

Use the "Examination of Conscience: Jesus, Heal Us" found on CD/CS–#16, mb–#20. If you cannot do the musical setting, use the text for the examination and a spoken response of "Jesus, Heal Us."

LORD'S PRAYER

Leader: Let us join in the words that Christ has given us.

All: **Our Father . . . for the kingdom, the power, and the glory are yours, now and for ever. Amen.**

CONCLUDING RITE

"Final Blessing," CD/CS–#19, mb–#25, or:

Leader: The Lord be with you.
All: **And also with you.**
Leader: May almighty God bless us, the Father, the Son, ✠ and the Holy Spirit.
All: **Amen!**
Leader: Our celebration has ended. Let us go forth to love and serve our God.
All: **Thanks be to God.**

Concluding Song

"Deep Down I Know," CD/CS–#10, mb–#12

The Christian Community

Getting Started

During this prayer service we will focus on the community prayer. Instead of a "ritual action" section we will extend the general intercessions. Encourage the students to think about issues in the world and their lives for which they can spontaneously pray.

INTRODUCTORY
RITES

Opening Song

"Deep Down I Know," CD/CS–#10, mb–#12

Leader: In the name of the Father, and of the Son, and of the Holy Spirit.
All: **Amen!**
Leader: The Lord be with you.
All: **And also with you.**

Opening Comments

Leader: As we gather in this Christmas Season, let us pray for the needs of this world. We are called to pray for the whole world as we pray for our own personal needs.

Opening Prayer

Leader: Let us pray. *(orans gesture)*
Lord Jesus,
we ask you to open our hearts to our Christian calling
to seek and find those who are forgotten, suffering, or poor,
so that we may bring them your love.
Help us be generous with our time,
our possessions, and ourselves
in your ministry of loving service.
We praise you as Christ our Lord. Amen!

SCRIPTURE
READING

1 Peter 3:15–18

A Bible should be on the prayer table. Reverence the Bible and then lift and read directly from it.

Leader: A reading from the First Letter of Peter.

Honor Christ and let him be the Lord of your life. Always be ready to give an answer when someone asks you about your hope. Give a kind and respectful answer and keep your conscience clear. This way you will make people ashamed for saying bad things about your good conduct as a follower of Christ. You are better off to obey God and suffer for doing right than to suffer for doing wrong. Christ died once for our sins. An innocent person died for those who are guilty. Christ did this to bring you to God, when his body was put to death and his spirit was made alive.

Leader: The word of the Lord.
All: **Thanks be to God.**

Reflection
Share with the group your feelings about the Scripture reading. Use these questions for your personal reflection.
1. *How can you best communicate to others your hope and faith in Jesus Christ?*
2. *When have you had to defend your commitment of being a Catholic?*
3. *How does the Holy Spirit help you in trying to live the life of a Catholic?*

Song
"Like the Sweet Fragrance" (Canticle of Sirach), CD/CS–#11, mb–#13

INTERCESSIONS "General Intercessions," in music collection or:

Leader: Let us come before God with our needs.

Reader: For the Church and all who serve the needs of people.
Let us pray to the Lord.
All: **Lord, hear our prayer.**

Reader: For all world leaders who work for peace. Let us pray to the Lord.

For those who feel unloved and in need of our concern.
Let us pray to the Lord.

Let us now voice our own petitions to God.

Insert your own intentions here.

For those who are sick and are in need of our prayers.
Let us pray to the Lord.

For those who have died. Let us pray to the Lord.

LORD'S PRAYER
Leader: Let us join in the words that Christ has given us.

All: **Our Father . . . for the kingdom, the power, and the glory are yours, now and for ever. Amen.**

CONCLUDING RITE "Final Blessing," CD/CS–#19, mb–#25, or:

Leader: The Lord be with you.
All: **And also with you.**
Leader: May almighty God bless us, the Father, the Son, ✠ and the Holy Spirit.

All: **Amen!**
Leader: Our celebration has ended. Let us go forth to love and serve our God.
All: **Thanks be to God.**

Concluding Song
"Blest Are You, O God" (Canticle of Zachary), CD/CS–#7, mb–#7

Faithful to the Covenant

UNIT 5
CHAPTERS 17–20

Getting Started

In this Season of Lent we seriously reflect on the choices we make in our lives. We will also repeat the examination of conscience. Review the Sacrament of Reconciliation with the students and remind them that during this season it is customary to take part in this sacrament.

INTRODUCTORY
RITES

Opening Song

"Blest Are They," CD/CS–#17, mb–#22

Leader:	In the name of the Father, and of the Son, and of the Holy Spirit.
All:	**Amen!**
Leader:	The Lord be with you.
All:	**And also with you.**

Opening Comments

Leader: We are entering into *(or are in)* the Season of Lent. This is a time for constant prayer. Let us reflect on the choices we will make during this Season of Lent. We are called to stay faithful to the covenant of God's love.

Opening Prayer

Leader: Let us pray. *(orans gesture)*
Lord,
you created us for yourself
and our hearts are restless until they rest in you.
Please show us how to love you with all our heart
and our neighbors as ourselves.
Teach us to be practical about loving one another
in you and for you and as you desire.
During this Season of Lent may we always
serve our brothers and sisters.
We ask this through Christ our Lord. Amen!

SCRIPTURE
READING

1 John 4:7–12

A Bible should be on the prayer table. Reverence the Bible and then lift and read directly from it.

Leader: A reading from the First Letter of John.

My dear friends, we must love each other. Love comes from God, and when we love each other, it shows that we have been given new life. We are now God's children, and we know him. God is love, and anyone who doesn't love others has never known him. God showed his love for us when he sent his only Son into the world to give us life. Real love isn't our love for God, but his love for us. God sent his Son to be the sacrifice by which our sins are forgiven. Dear friends, since God loved us this much, we must love each other. No one has ever seen God. But if we love each other, God lives in us, and his love is truly in our hearts.

Leader: The word of the Lord.
All: **Thanks be to God.**

Reflection

Share with the group your feelings about the Scripture reading. Use these questions for your personal reflection.

1. *How do you feel the presence of God in the action of loving others?*
2. *During Lent, what discipline of prayer do you practice?*
3. *What can you do this Lenten Season to help those in your community?*

Song

"Lord, Be with Me" (Psalm 91), CD/CS–#14, mb–#17

RITUAL ACTION
Use the "Examination of Conscience: Jesus, Heal Us," CD/CS–#16, mb–#20, or the ritual in the student textbook, page 133.

LORD'S PRAYER
Leader: Let us join in the words that Christ has given us.

All: **Our Father . . . for the kingdom, the power, and the glory are yours, now and for ever. Amen.**

CONCLUDING RITE
"Final Blessing," CD/CS–#19, mb–#25, or:

Leader: The Lord be with you.
All: **And also with you.**
Leader: May almighty God bless us, the Father, the Son, ✠ and the Holy Spirit.
All: **Amen!**
Leader: Our celebration has ended. Let us go forth to love and serve our God.
All: **Thanks be to God.**

Concluding Song

"Deep Down I Know," CD/CS–#10, mb–#12

Celebrating the Sacraments

UNIT 6
CHAPTERS 21–24

Getting Started

During this ritual we will reflect on Holy Week and the apostles' response to God's call. We do this by carrying out a washing of the feet in the classroom. Although this ritual is done on Holy Thursday, the action may have more meaning for children this age if first done in a catechetical setting. To do this you need warm water with some lemon extract added to it. Have a few basins and a few pitchers. You will also need many towels. Have the children bring one from home to donate to the parish or ask the parish sacristan if there is a large quantity used at Holy Thursday which you could borrow. Select some students to pour the water over the feet. As the catechist, you may wish to invite other adults to help you—the principal, DRE, or the students' family members. Yes, the first time you do this it will seem strange and the students may laugh, but that is OK. If the leaders are reverent, the rite will have a powerful effect on the students during Holy Thursday. You will need to reflect on this rite afterwards. Be sure to answer how you felt during the experience.

INTRODUCTORY RITES

Opening Song

"Lord, Be with Me" (Psalm 91), CD/CS–#14, mb–#17

Leader: In the name of the Father, and of the Son, and of the Holy Spirit.
All: **Amen!**
Leader: The Lord be with you.
All: **And also with you.**

Opening Comments

Leader: As we gather this day we are called to serve the needs of others. Today we will hear of something special Jesus did with his apostles. He chose to serve his friends. Let us take some time to reflect on our lives and how we can be of service to our neighbors.

Opening Prayer

Leader: Let us pray. *(orans gesture)*
God our Father,
you made us your children
by water and the Holy Spirit.
Bless us and watch over us with fatherly love.
Jesus Christ, Son of God,
you promised that the Spirit of truth
would be with your Church for ever.
Bless us and give us courage
in professing the true faith.
Holy Spirit, you came down upon the disciples
and set their hearts on fire with love.
Bless us, and keep us one in faith and love.
We ask this through Christ our Lord. Amen!

SCRIPTURE
READING

John 13:4–8

A Bible should be on the prayer table. Reverence the Bible and then lift and read directly from it.

Leader: The Lord be with you.

All: **And also with you.**

Leader: A reading from the holy Gospel according to John.

All: **Glory to you, O Lord.**

During a meal Jesus got up, removed his outer garment, and wrapped a towel around his waist. He put some water into a large bowl. Then he began washing his disciples' feet and drying them with the towel he was wearing. But when he came to Simon Peter, that disciple asked, "Lord, are you going to wash my feet?" Jesus answered, "You don't really know what I am doing, but later you will understand." "You will never wash my feet!" Peter replied. "If I don't wash you," Jesus told him, "you don't really belong to me."

Leader: The gospel of the Lord.

All: **Praise to you, Lord Jesus Christ.**

Reflection

Share with the group your feelings about the Scripture reading. Use these questions for your personal reflection.

1. *What would it have been like to have your own feet washed by Jesus?*
2. *What does it mean for you to wash feet? Why would you wash someone's feet?*
3. *Whose feet are you asked to wash?*
4. *Who has washed feet in this world? Reflect on the life of Mother Teresa.*

Song

"Like the Sweet Fragrance" (Canticle of Sirach), CD/CS–#11, mb–#13

RITUAL ACTION

Leader: We are now going to do as the Scripture said. As a class we will wash feet. It may seem strange, but remember Christ's call to his apostles. *During this time you may need many adults to help you, and you may need to combine a few classes together to save time. See specific instructions above. Also inquire into how the parish washes feet on Holy Thursday. Use this procedure as your model.*

LORD'S PRAYER

Leader: Let us join in the words that Christ has given us.

All: **Our Father . . . for the kingdom, the power, and the glory are yours, now and for ever. Amen.**

CONCLUDING RITE "Final Blessing," CD/CS–#19, mb–#25, or:

Leader: The Lord be with you.
All: **And also with you.**
Leader: May almighty God bless us, the Father, the Son, ✠ and the Holy Spirit.
All: **Amen!**
Leader: Our celebration has ended. Let us go forth to love and serve our God.
All: **Thanks be to God.**

Concluding Song
"Prayer for Peace," CD/CS–#13, mb–#16

The Love that Never Ends

UNIT 7
CHAPTERS 25–28

Getting Started

As the catechetical year comes to an end, this would be a good time to review where you have been this year. Review highlights of each of the seven prayer rituals. Review how they connected to the ideas of making choices and praising God. This ritual works well when done around the Easter baptismal font. If possible, gather around the parish font. If not, bring holy water from church and pour it into a large bowl, light a candle, and gather.

INTRODUCTORY RITES

Opening Song

"Alleluia/Gospel Acclamation," CD/CS–#5, mb–#5

Leader: In the name of the Father, and of the Son, and of the Holy Spirit.
All: **Amen!**
Leader: The Lord be with you.
All: **And also with you.**

Opening Comments

Leader: We come to the end of another year. The Church celebrates new life during this Easter Season. We too celebrate new life, for we have journeyed as people of faith this year. Let us celebrate our call to make good choices in the name of Jesus Christ.

Opening Prayer

Leader: Let us pray. *(orans gesture)*
All-powerful God of love,
you raised our Lord Jesus Christ
from death to life,
shining in glory as the King of creation.
Open our hearts,
free all the world to rejoice in his peace,
to glory in his justice, to live in his love.
Bring all people together.
We ask this through Christ our Lord. Amen!

SCRIPTURE READING

Matthew 5:43–48

A Bible should be on the prayer table. Reverence the Bible and then lift and read directly from it.

Leader: The Lord be with you.
All: **And also with you.**
Leader: A reading from the holy Gospel according to Matthew.
All: **Glory to you, O Lord.**

You have heard people say, "Love your neighbors and hate your enemies." But I tell you to love your enemies and pray for anyone who mistreats you. Then you will be acting like your Father in heaven. He makes the sun rise on both good and bad people. And he sends rain for the ones who do right and for the ones who do wrong. If you love only those people who love you, will God reward you for that? Even tax collectors love their friends. If you greet only your friends, what's so great about that? Don't even unbelievers do that? But you must always act like your Father in heaven.

Leader: The gospel of the Lord.

All: **Praise to you, Lord Jesus Christ.**

Reflection

Share with the group your feelings about the Scripture reading. Use these questions for your personal reflection.

1. *As you come to the end of this year, how has your feeling of love for God and others changed?*
2. *What stories of faith can you share from this year about making choices and doing the will of God?*
3. *What challenges you in living as a moral Christian?*

Song

"This Is the Day" (Psalm 118), CD/CS–#12, mb–#14

RITUAL ACTION

Renewal of Baptismal Promises

If possible, gather around the parish font or use holy water from the parish. If not, gather in a circle and end the ritual by having each student sign one another with the Sign of the Cross.

Leader: Do you reject evil and renew your commitment to Jesus Christ?

All: **I do.**

Leader: Do you believe in God, the Father almighty, creator of heaven and earth?

All: **I do.**

Leader: Do you believe in Jesus Christ, Son of God?

All: **I do.**

Leader: Do you believe in the Holy Spirit?

All: **I do.**

Leader: Will you proclaim by word and example the good news of God in Christ?

All: **I will, with God's help.**

Leader: Will you strive for justice and peace among all people?

All: **I will, with God's help.**

Leader: *(if water is present)* Let us come to the Easter waters and sign one another.

LORD'S PRAYER

Leader: Let us join in the words that Christ has given us.

All: **Our Father . . . for the kingdom, the power, and the glory are yours, now and for ever. Amen.**

CONCLUDING RITE

"Final Blessing," CD/CS–#19, mb–#25, or:

Leader: The Lord be with you.
All: **And also with you.**
Leader: May almighty God bless us, the Father, the Son, ✠ and the Holy Spirit.
All: **Amen!**
Leader: Our celebration has ended. Let us go forth to love and serve our God.
All: **Thanks be to God.**

Concluding Song
"Walking by Faith," CD/CS–#1, mb–#1

Creation Celebrates God's Love

UNIT 1
CHAPTER 1–4

Getting Started

This prayer service celebrates our call to help each other. At the beginning of the year, use common responses and music that will be used at the first gathering of the school- or parish-wide liturgy.

INTRODUCTORY RITES

Opening Song

"Walking by Faith," CD/CS–#1, mb–#1

Leader: In the name of the Father, and of the Son, and of the Holy Spirit.
All: **Amen!**
Leader: The Lord be with you.
All: **And also with you.**

Opening Comments

Leader: As we begin our new school year, let us offer to help one another. May our hearts and hands work together as we learn about God's love this year.

Opening Prayer

Leader: Let us pray. *(orans gesture)*
God our Creator,
we are the work of your hands.
Guide us in our work,
that we may do it, not for self alone,
but for the common good.
Make us alert to injustice,
ready to stand in solidarity,
that there may be dignity for all
in labor and in labor's reward.
We ask this through Christ our Lord. Amen!

SCRIPTURE READING

Matthew 6:31–33

A Bible should be on the prayer table. Reverence the Bible and then lift and read directly from it.

Leader: The Lord be with you.
All: **And also with you.**
Leader: A reading from the holy Gospel according to Matthew.
All: **Glory to you, O Lord.**

Don't worry and ask yourselves, "Will we have anything to eat? Will we have anything to drink? Will we have any clothes to wear?" Only people who don't know God are always worrying about such things. Your Father in heaven knows that you need all of these. But more than anything else, put

God's work first and do what he wants. Then the other things will be yours as well.

Leader: The gospel of the Lord.
All: **Praise to you, Lord Jesus Christ.**

Reflection
Share with the group your feelings about the Scripture reading. Use these questions for your personal reflection.
1. *When have you put absolute trust in God?*
2. *How difficult was this trust for you?*
3. *What is the work of God that is the basis of your life?*

Song
"Holy Is Your Name" (Canticle of Mary), CD/CS–#4, mb–#4

RITUAL ACTION
Leader: I invite each student to come forward and open your hands as we pray together.
As the students come up, place your hands on theirs, saying, "N., I pray that you will allow God's love to shine through you. Amen!"

INTERCESSIONS
"General Intercessions," in music collection or:

Leader: Let us come before God with our needs.

Reader: For our Church and all who show us how to trust in God.
Let us pray to the Lord.
All: **Lord, hear our prayer.**

Reader: For peace in our world and in our homes. Let us pray to the Lord.

For all of us as we share in God's love this year. Let us pray to the Lord.

Add your own intentions here.

For those who are sick and ask for God's healing touch.
Let us pray to the Lord.

For those who have died and live with God for ever.
Let us pray to the Lord.

LORD'S PRAYER
Leader: Let us join in the words that Christ has given us.

All: **Our Father . . . for the kingdom, the power, and the glory are yours, now and for ever. Amen.**

CONCLUDING RITE   "Final Blessing," CD/CS–#19, mb–#25, or:

Leader: The Lord be with you.
All: **And also with you.**
Leader: May almighty God bless us, the Father, the Son, ✠ and the Holy Spirit.
All: **Amen!**
Leader: Our celebration has ended. Let us go forth to love and serve our God.
All: **Thanks be to God.**

Concluding Song
"Deep Down I Know," CD/CS–#10, mb–#12

We Worship Our God

Getting Started

It is suggested for this prayer service that we celebrate a washing of the feet. Although unusual, it will enhance our call to service. To do this you need warm water with lemon extract. Have a few basins and pitchers handy. You will also need a lot of towels. Have the children bring one from home to donate to the parish or ask the parish sacristan if there are large quantities available for use from Holy Thursday. Select some students to pour the water over the feet. As the catechist, you may wish to invite other adults to help you–the principal, DRE, or the student's family members. Yes, the first time you do this it will be strange and the students may laugh, but that is OK. If you repeat this ritual a few times throughout the year, there will be a high reverence when the children come to the Holy Thursday celebration.

INTRODUCTORY
RITES

Opening Song

"God's People" (Psalm 100), CD/CS–#2, mb–#2

Leader: In the name of the Father, and of the Son, and of the Holy Spirit.
All: **Amen!**
Leader: The Lord be with you.
All: **And also with you.**

Opening Comments

Leader: As we gather in prayer and worship of our God, we remember our call to love and serve each other.

Opening Prayer

Leader: Let us pray. *(orans gesture)*
God our Father,
You gather us into your Church to be one,
as you, Father, are one with your Son and the Holy Spirit.
You call us to be your people,
to praise your wisdom in all your works.
You make us the Body of Christ
and the dwelling-place of the Holy Spirit.
May we always praise you with Christ our Lord. Amen!

SCRIPTURE
READING

John 13:4–8

A Bible should be on the prayer table. Reverence the Bible and then lift and read directly from it.

Leader: A reading from the holy Gospel according to John.
All: **Glory to you, O Lord.**

During a meal Jesus got up, removed his outer garment, and wrapped a towel around his waist. He put some water into a large bowl. Then he began washing his disciples' feet and drying them with the towel he was wearing. But when he came to Simon Peter, that disciple asked, "Lord, are you going to wash my feet?" Jesus answered, "You don't really know what I am doing, but later you will understand." "You will never wash my feet!" Peter replied. "If I don't wash you," Jesus told him, "you don't really belong to me."

Leader: The gospel of the Lord.
All: **Praise to you, Lord Jesus Christ.**

Reflection
Share with the group your feelings about the Scripture reading. Use these questions for your personal reflection.
1. *What would it have been like to have your own feet washed by Jesus?*
2. *What does it mean for you to wash feet? Why would you wash someone's feet?*
3. *Whose feet are you asked to wash?*
4. *Who has washed feet in our world? Reflect on the life of Mother Teresa.*

Song
"Blest Are You, O God" (Canticle of Zachary), CD/CS–#7, mb–#7

Ritual Action

Leader: We are now going to do as the Scripture said. As a class we will wash feet. It may seem strange, but remember Christ's call to his apostles. *During this time you may need many adults to help you, and you may need to combine a few classes together to save time. See specific instructions above. Also inquire into how the parish washes feet on Holy Thursday. Use this as a model.*

Intercessions

"General Intercessions," in music collection or:

Leader: Let us come before God with our needs.

Reader: For our Church and all the saints who have served us.
Let us pray to the Lord.
All: **Lord, hear our prayer.**

Reader: For the world and our call to serve people who are poor and needy.
Let us pray to the Lord.

For our own class as we continue our journey of faith and prayer.
Let us pray to the Lord.

Add your own intentions here.

For those who are sick and need the healing touch of Jesus.
Let us pray to the Lord.

For those who have died and now sit at the feast with Christ in heaven.
Let us pray to the Lord.

LORD'S PRAYER

Leader: Let us join in the words that Christ has given us.

All: **Our Father . . . for the kingdom, the power, and the glory are yours, now and for ever. Amen.**

CONCLUDING RITE

"Final Blessing," CD/CS–#19, mb–#25, or:

Leader: The Lord be with you.
All: **And also with you.**
Leader: May almighty God bless us, the Father, the Son, ✠ and the Holy Spirit.
All: **Amen!**
Leader: Our celebration has ended. Let us go forth to love and serve our God.
All: **Thanks be to God.**

Concluding Song
"Walking by Faith," CD/CS–#1, mb–#1

Jesus Is a Sacrament

UNIT 3
CHAPTERS 9–12

Getting Started

During this service we come to know God through Jesus, his words in Scripture, and the Paschal mystery of his dying and rising. In this service each student should receive a Scripture book. Inexpensive Bibles can be purchased from the American Bible Society, 1865 Broadway, New York, NY 10023. Their phone number is 1-800-32-BIBLE. This rite is also celebrated with catechumens and candidates as they enter into our faith.

INTRODUCTORY
RITES

Opening Song

Advent Gathering: "Make Ready the Way," CD/CS–#3, mb–#3

Leader: In the name of the Father, and of the Son, and of the Holy Spirit.
All: **Amen!**
Leader: The Lord be with you.
All: **And also with you.**

Opening Comments

Leader: In our lessons we come to know God through Jesus, his words in Scripture, and in the mystery of Christ's dying and rising. Let us be attentive to the way Christ is alive in our lives.

Opening Prayer

Leader: Let us pray. *(orans gesture)*
O God,
help us spread your love everywhere.
Shine through us, and be so much in us
that everyone with whom we come in contact
may feel your presence within us.
Let them look at us and in us see you.
We ask this through Christ our Lord. Amen!

SCRIPTURE
READING

Romans 6:3–8

A Bible should be on the prayer table. Reverence the Bible and then lift and read directly from it.

Leader: A reading from the Letter of Paul to the Romans.

Don't you know that all who share in Christ Jesus by being baptized also share in his death? When we were baptized, we died and were buried with Christ. We were baptized, so that we would live a new life, as Christ was raised to life by the glory of God the Father. If we shared in Jesus' death by being baptized, we will be raised to life with him. We know that the persons we used to be were nailed to the cross with Jesus. This was done, so that our sinful bodies would no longer be the slaves of sin. We know that sin doesn't have power over dead people. As surely as we died with Christ, we believe we will also live with him.

Leader: The word of the Lord.
All: **Thanks be to God.**

Reflection

Share with the group your feelings about the Scripture reading. Use these questions for your personal reflection.
  1. *What would your life be like or what was your life like without Jesus?*
  2. *What does it mean to you to have a new life in Jesus?*
  3. *What Scripture stories bring you closer to God?*
  4. *What sacrament do you most identify with or what sacrament brings you closer to God?*

Song

"Holy Is Your Name" (Canticle of Mary), CD/CS–#4, mb–#4, or
"To You, O Lord" (Psalm 25), CD/CS–#6, mb–#6

RITUAL ACTION   *Invite each student to come forward. Have them either place a hand on the Bible or give each of them a Bible, saying, "N., may the word of God be active and alive in your heart and in your life. Amen!"*

hand on bible

INTERCESSIONS   "General Intercessions," in music collection or:

Leader: Let us come before God with our needs.

Reader: For the Church and all who live the message of God's love.
Let us pray to the Lord.
All: **Lord, hear our prayer.**

Reader: For the world and all who live by the message of peace.
Let us pray to the Lord.

For each of us as we reflect on God's love which is present in the words of Christ. Let us pray to the Lord.

Insert your own intentions here.

For those who are ill and ask for God's healing love.
Let us pray to the Lord.

For those who have died and are now rejoicing in heaven.
Let us pray to the Lord.

LORD'S PRAYER

Leader: Let us join in the words that Christ has given us.

All: **Our Father . . . for the kingdom, the power, and the glory are yours, now and for ever. Amen.**

CONCLUDING RITE

"Final Blessing," CD/CS–#19, mb–#25, or:

Leader: The Lord be with you.
All: **And also with you.**
Leader: May almighty God bless us, the Father, the Son, ✠ and the Holy Spirit.
All: **Amen!**
Leader: Our celebration has ended. Let us go forth to love and serve our God.
All: **Thanks be to God.**

Concluding Song
"Prayer for Peace," CD/CS–#13, mb–#16

The Church Is a Sacrament

**UNIT 4
CHAPTERS 13–16**

Getting Started

It's the beginning of a new calendar year. During this service we pray for unity among Christians. We also have a celebration over water already blessed. Use a large bowl of holy water from church, and when saying the invocations, move your hand through the water and lift it up so that a sound of water is heard.

**INTRODUCTORY
RITES**

Opening Song

"God's People" (Psalm 100), CD/CS–#2, mb–#2

Leader: In the name of the Father, and of the Son, and of the Holy Spirit.
All: **Amen!**
Leader: The Lord be with you.
All: **And also with you.**

Opening Comments

Leader: As we begin this new year we remember our baptismal call to love and serve all people. We remember in a special way Christians throughout the world. It is with all of God's faithful that we form the Body of Christ.

Opening Prayer

Leader: Let us pray. *(orans gesture)*
Almighty and eternal God,
you gather the scattered sheep
and watch over those you have gathered.
Look kindly on all who follow Jesus, your Son.
You have marked them with the seal of one Baptism,
now make them one in the fullness of faith
and unite them in the bond of love.
We ask this through Christ our Lord. Amen!

**SCRIPTURE
READING**

Mark 1:9–11

A Bible should be on the prayer table. Reverence the Bible and then lift and read directly from it.

Leader: The Lord be with you.
All: **And also with you.**
Leader: A reading from the holy Gospel according to Mark.
All: **Glory to you, O Lord.**

Jesus came from Nazareth in Galilee, and John baptized him in the Jordan River. As soon as Jesus came out of the water, he saw the sky open and the Holy Spirit coming down to him like a dove. A voice from heaven said, "You are my own dear Son, and I am pleased with you."

Leader: The gospel of the Lord.
All: **Praise to you, Lord Jesus Christ.**

Reflection

Share with the group your feelings about the Scripture reading. Use these questions for your personal reflection.

1. *What would it have been like to be present at the Baptism of Christ?*
2. *When in your life did you recognize Jesus as the "Son of God"?*
3. *For you, how is the water used in Baptism different from everyday water?*
4. *How does the Holy Spirit infuse your life to do good works?*

Song

"Blest Are You, O God" (Canticle of Zachary), CD/CS–#7, mb–#7

RITUAL ACTION

Use "Greeting and Thanksgiving Over Water Already Blessed" from "People of God/Alleluia," CD/CS–#8, mb–#8, or the following:

Leader: God our Father, you give us grace through sacramental signs which tell us of the wonders of your unseen power. Please respond, "Blessed are you, O Lord our God!"

Move hand through water during invocations.

At the dawn of creation, your Spirit breathed on the waters. *Response.*

You made the waters of the great flood a sign of the end of sin. *Response.*

Through the waters of the Red Sea, you led Israel out of slavery. *Response.*

In the waters of the Jordan, your Son was baptized by John and anointed by the Spirit. *Response.*

Water and blood flowed from Jesus' side as he hung on the cross. *Response.*

In the Sacrament of Baptism, may all those you have created in your likeness be cleansed from sin and risen to new birth by water and the Holy Spirit. Amen.

I invite everyone to come forward and sign themselves with these waters.

The leader blesses himself or herself, making the Sign of the Cross with the holy water. Then the students do the same.

INTERCESSIONS   "General Intercessions," in music collection or:

Leader: Let us come before God with our needs.

Reader: For the Church and all people who believe in God.
Let us pray to the Lord.
All: **Lord, hear our prayer.**

Reader: For our country and all people seeking peace. Let us pray to the Lord.

For those who feel unloved and on the outside of life.
Let us pray to the Lord.

Add your own intentions here.

For those who are sick and seek the healing touch of Christ.
Let us pray to the Lord.

For those who have died and now celebrate eternal life with Christ.
Let us pray to the Lord.

LORD'S PRAYER
Leader: Let us join in the words that Christ has given us.

All: **Our Father . . . for the kingdom, the power, and the glory are yours,
now and for ever. Amen.**

CONCLUDING RITE   "Final Blessing," CD/CS–#19, mb–#25, or:

Leader: The Lord be with you.
All: **And also with you.**
Leader: May almighty God bless us, the Father, the Son, ✠ and the Holy Spirit.
All: **Amen!**
Leader: Our celebration has ended. Let us go forth to love and serve our God.
All: **Thanks be to God.**

Concluding Song
"Prayer for Peace," CD/CS–#13, mb–#16

The Life of Grace

UNIT 5
CHAPTERS 17–20

Getting Started

During this unit we reflect on our need to admit our own wrongdoings. Here we incorporate an examination of conscience. You may want to show the video, "A Father and Two Sons" by the American Bible Society and distributed by BROWN-ROA. This video could be helpful as a prelude to this prayer celebration. Encourage students to attend the Sacrament of Reconciliation.

INTRODUCTORY RITES

Opening Song
"Prayer for Peace," CD/CS–#13, mb–#16

Leader: In the name of the Father, and of the Son, and of the Holy Spirit.
All: **Amen!**
Leader: The Lord be with you.
All: **And also with you.**

Opening Comments

Leader: We gather remembering that we make mistakes. Within our mistakes God hears us and answers us. Let us have the courage to look at ourselves and trust in the love of God.

Opening Prayer

Leader: Let us pray. *(orans gesture)*
Lord of mercy,
you have made all things with your word.
Give us wisdom,
for she knows and understands all things,
and will guide us in our choices, and keep us safe.
Then our actions will be acceptable to you.
Our way will be clear and our path will be straight,
and we will be saved.
We ask this through Christ our Lord. Amen!

SCRIPTURE READING

Luke 15:11–24
A Bible should be on the prayer table. Reverence the Bible and then lift and read directly from it.
Leader: The Lord be with you.
All: **And also with you.**
Leader: A reading from the holy Gospel according to Luke.
All: **Glory to you, O Lord.**

Jesus told the crowds a story:
Once a man had two sons. The younger son said to his father, "Give me my share of the property." So the father divided his property between his two sons. Not long after that, the younger son packed up everything he owned and left for a foreign country, where he wasted all his money in wild living.

He had spent everything, when a bad famine spread through that whole land. Soon he had nothing to eat.

He went to work for a man in that country, and the man sent him out to take care of his pigs. He would have been glad to eat what the pigs were eating, but no one gave him a thing. Finally, he came to his senses and said, "My father's workers have plenty to eat, and here I am, starving to death! I will go to my father and say to him, 'Father, I have sinned against God in heaven and against you. I am no longer good enough to be called your son. Treat me like one of your workers.'"

The younger son got up and started back to his father. But when he was still a long way off, his father saw him and felt sorry for him. He ran to his son and hugged and kissed him. The son said, "Father, I have sinned against God in heaven and against you. I am no longer good enough to be called your son."

But his father said to the servants, "Hurry and bring the best clothes and put them on him. Give him a ring for his finger and sandals for his feet. Get the best calf and prepare it, so we can eat and celebrate. This son of mine was dead, but has now come back to life. He was lost and has now been found." And they began to celebrate.

Leader: The gospel of the Lord.
All: **Praise to you, Lord Jesus Christ.**

Reflection
Share with the group your feelings about the Scripture reading. Use these questions for your personal reflection.
1. *How hard would it have been for you to return to your parent and ask forgiveness?*
2. *When in your own life have you felt the healing love of God?*
3. *What in your own life will you have to do to freely forgive others?*

Song
"Lord, Be with Me" (Psalm 91), CD/CS–#14, mb–#17

RITUAL ACTION   *Use "Examination of Conscience: Jesus, Heal Us," CD/CS–#16, mb–#20, or the following text:*

Leader: Please respond, "Hear us and heal us, O God."
God our Father, sometimes we have not behaved as your children. *Response.*

We have given trouble to our family members and teachers. *Response.*

We have quarreled and called each other names. *Response.*

We have been lazy at home or in school, and we have not been helpful to our families and our friends. *Response.*

We have thought too much of ourselves and have told lies. *Response.*

We have not done good to others when we had the chance. *Response.*

Leader: Let us kneel and ask God for forgiveness.

All: **I confess to almighty God,
and to you, my brothers and sisters,
that I have sinned through my own fault
in my thoughts and in my words,
in what I have done,
and in what I have failed to do;
and I ask blessed Mary, ever virgin,
all the angels and saints,
and you, my brothers and sisters,
to pray for me to the Lord our God.**

LORD'S PRAYER

Leader: Let us stand and join in the words that Jesus gave us.

All: **Our Father . . . for the kingdom, the power, and the glory are yours,
now and for ever. Amen.**

CONCLUDING RITE

"Final Blessing," CD/CS–#19, mb–#25, or:

Leader: The Lord be with you.
All: **And also with you.**
Leader: May almighty God bless us, the Father, the Son, ✠ and the Holy Spirit.
All: **Amen!**
Leader: Our celebration has ended. Let us go forth to love and serve our God.
All: **Thanks be to God.**

Concluding Song
"Walking by Faith," CD/CS–#1, mb–#1

The Eucharist, Our Great Sacrament

Getting Started

We celebrate this service sometime close to Easter. It would be appropriate to venerate a cross. You may want to show the students how to make a profound bow before a cross. Do this either with the parish cross in church or use the cross from the classroom. If you can use a large cross or the parish processional cross, have one of the students hold the cross and face different groups of students around the room. When the cross is facing a group, the students are to bow. Ask someone from the parish liturgy committee to come in to speak to the students on the procedure for the veneration of the cross on Good Friday.

INTRODUCTORY RITES

Opening Song

"Song of the Body of Christ," CD/CS–#18, mb–#24

Leader: In the name of the Father, and of the Son, and of the Holy Spirit.
All: **Amen!**
Leader: The Lord be with you.
All: **And also with you.**

Opening Comments

Leader: We gather and remember how Jesus is the Bread of Life. We also recall that by his cross he calls us to serve the Church. We must come before the cross and pass through its pain into the glory in Christ's world all around us.

Opening Prayer

Leader: Let us pray. *(orans gesture)*
God our Father,
open our eyes to see your hand at work
in the splendor of creation, and in the beauty of human life.
Touched by your hand, our world is holy.
Help us cherish the gifts that surround us,
share your blessings with our brothers and sisters,
and experience the joy of life in your presence.
We ask this through Christ our Lord. Amen!

SCRIPTURE READING

2 Timothy 3:12, 14–17

A Bible should be on the prayer table. Reverence the Bible and then lift and read directly from it.

Leader: A reading from Paul's Second Letter to Timothy.

Anyone who belongs to Christ Jesus and wants to live right will have trouble from others. Keep on being faithful to what you were taught and to what you believed. After all, you know who taught you these things. Since childhood, you have known the Holy Scriptures that are able to make you wise enough to have faith in Christ Jesus and be saved. Everything in the Scriptures is God's Word. All of it is useful for teaching and helping people and for correcting them and showing them how to live. The Scriptures train God's servants to do all kinds of good deeds.

Leader: The word of the Lord.
All: **Thanks be to God.**

Reflection
Share with the group your feelings about the Scripture reading. Use these questions for your personal reflection.
1. *What have you been taught from Scripture that has helped you in your spiritual journey?*
2. *Which Scripture passage speaks of your spiritual journey right now?*
3. *What challenges you in living the gospel truths?*

Song
"Raining Down Manna" (Psalm 78), CD/CS–#15, mb–#19

RITUAL ACTION **Veneration of the Cross** *(See notes above.)*
Leader: On Good Friday our Church venerates the cross of Jesus. We recognize how Christ died on the cross so that we all could share in his resurrection. In silence, let us reverence the cross and ask God to be with us as we face our own struggles in this world.
Venerate the cross here.

INTERCESSIONS "General Intercessions," in music collection or:

Leader: Let us come before God with our needs.

Reader: For our Church and all who are asked to carry the cross of Jesus.
Let us pray to the Lord.
All: **Lord, hear our prayer.**

Reader: For leaders of this world who are asked to carry the banner of peace.
Let us pray to the Lord.

For those who feel the cross of poverty is too great to carry.
Let us pray to the Lord.

Insert your own personal intentions here.

For those who are ill and ask for the healing touch of Christ.
Let us pray to the Lord.

For those who have died and now live in the glory of Christ.
Let us pray to the Lord.

LORD'S PRAYER

Leader: Let us join in the words that Christ has given us.

All: **Our Father . . . for the kingdom, the power, and the glory are yours, now and for ever. Amen.**

CONCLUDING RITE

"Final Blessing," CD/CS–#19, mb–#25, or:

Leader: The Lord be with you.
All: **And also with you.**
Leader: May almighty God bless us, the Father, the Son, ✠ and the Holy Spirit.
All: **Amen!**
Leader: Our celebration has ended. Let us go forth to love and serve our God.
All: **Thanks be to God.**

Concluding Song
"Deep Down I Know," CD/CS–#10, mb–#12

The Paschal Mystery

UNIT 7
CHAPTERS 25–28

Getting Started

This prayer service is done in the final weeks of catechesis. During this time you may want to invite a newly initiated member of the parish in to share his or her own experiences of becoming Catholic. The students will also renew their baptismal promises. It would be nice to do this service around the parish baptismal font. If not, see if you can use some water from the font in your catechetical setting. After the renewal of promises, have the students sign one another with the holy water.

INTRODUCTORY
RITES

Opening Song

Verses 1 and 2 from "People of God/Alleluia," CD/CS–#8, mb–#8

Leader: In the name of the Father, and of the Son, and of the Holy Spirit.
All: **Amen!**
Leader: The Lord be with you.
All: **And also with you.**

Opening Comments

Leader: We gather in this Easter Season to celebrate all the good things God has done. Let us rejoice and be glad.

Opening Prayer

Leader: Let us pray. *(orans gesture)*
Good and gracious God,
at the heavenly banquet in the new Jerusalem,
Jesus the Lamb of God will spread a table and feed us.
He is our Beginning and End.
Then we shall come to know God in a vision so blessed
that we will know as we are known.
We praise you as the God who lives and reigns for ever and ever.
Amen. Alleluia!

SCRIPTURE
READING

1 Corinthians 13:1, 4–8, 11, 13

A Bible should be on the prayer table. Reverence the Bible and then lift and read directly from it.

Leader: A reading from the First Letter of Paul to the Corinthians.

What if I could speak all languages of humans and of angels? If I did not love others, I would be nothing more than a noisy gong or a clanging cymbal. Love is kind and patient, never jealous, boastful, proud, or rude. Love isn't selfish or quick tempered. It doesn't keep a record of wrongs that others do. Love rejoices in the truth, but not in evil. Love is always supportive, loyal, hopeful, and trusting. Love never fails! Everyone who prophesies will stop, and unknown languages will no longer be spoken. All that we know will be forgotten. When we were children, we thought and reasoned as children do. But when we grew up, we quit our childish ways.

For now there are faith, hope, and love. But of these three, the greatest is love.

Leader: The word of the Lord.
All: **Thanks be to God.**

Reflection
Share with the group your feelings about the Scripture reading. Use these questions for your personal reflection.
1. *What is your experience of the different descriptions of love in this reading?*
2. *Who in your life showed you the love of God?*
3. *How has your love for others matured from "childish" ways to that of "adult" ways?*
4. *What challenges do you face in the world when choosing to live as a person of love?*

Song
"This Is the Day" (Psalm 118), CD/CS–#12, mb–#14

RITUAL ACTION   **Renewal of Baptismal Promises**
If possible, gather around the parish font or use holy water from the parish. If not, gather in a circle and end the baptismal promises by having each student sign one another with the Sign of the Cross.

Leader: Do you reject evil and renew your commitment to Jesus Christ?
All: **I do.**

Leader: Do you believe in God, the Father almighty, creator of heaven and earth?
All: **I do.**

Leader: Do you believe in Jesus Christ, Son of God?
All: **I do.**

Leader: Do you believe in the Holy Spirit?
All: **I do.**

Leader: Will you proclaim by word and example the good news of God in Christ?
All: **I will, with God's help.**

Leader: Will you strive for justice and peace among all people?
All: **I will, with God's help.**

Leader: *(if water is present)* Let us come to the Easter waters and sign one another.

LORD'S PRAYER

Leader: Let us join in the words that Christ has given us.

All: **Our Father . . . for the kingdom, the power, and the glory are yours, now and for ever. Amen.**

CONCLUDING RITE

"Final Blessing," CD/CS–#19, mb–#25, or:

Leader: The Lord be with you.
All: **And also with you.**
Leader: May almighty God bless us, the Father, the Son, ✠ and the Holy Spirit.
All: **Amen!**
Leader: Our celebration has ended. Let us go forth to love and serve our God.
All: **Thanks be to God.**

Concluding Song
"Walking by Faith," CD/CS–#1, mb–#1

In the Beginning

UNIT 1
CHAPTERS 1–4

Getting Started

This year we will be making commitments to be of service to others. Choose one charity or local need, and contribute to it at each service. If you choose a food pantry, have a collection of food at each service. If you choose to give money to a local shelter, collect it at each service. Talk to someone in your parish who may be involved with social justice needs. They can direct your students' efforts toward something concrete. These actions can be done simply but they should be done with an attitude of genuine service to other people.

INTRODUCTORY RITES

Opening Song

"Walking by Faith," CD/CS–#1, mb–#1

Leader: In the name of the Father, and of the Son, and of the Holy Spirit.
All: **Amen!**
Leader: The Lord be with you.
All: **And also with you.**

Opening Comments

Leader: As we begin this new year together, let us remember our call to serve each other in love. Let us always remember those who are not as fortunate as us, and let us always remember our call to be part of the larger world of humanity.

Opening Prayer

Leader: Let us pray. *(orans gesture)*
Almighty and ever-living God,
you have made us stewards over the created world,
so that in all things we might honor the demands of charity.
Empower us to use our gifts to serve the needs of our neighbors.
May we serve all of humanity with upright hearts.
We ask this through Christ our Lord. Amen!

SCRIPTURE READING

1 John 4:12, 19–21

A Bible should be on the prayer table. Reverence the Bible and then lift and read directly from it.

Leader: A reading from the First Letter of John.

No one has ever seen God. But if we love each other, God lives in us, and his love is truly in our hearts. We love because God loved us first. But if we say we love God and don't love each other, we are liars. We cannot see God. So how can we love God, if we don't love the people we can see? The commandment that God has given us is: "Love God and love each other!"

Leader: The word of the Lord.
All: **Thanks be to God.**

Reflection

Share with the group your feelings about the Scripture reading. Use these questions for your personal reflection.

1. *What does the word "love" mean for you, as used in this Scripture?*
2. *Who in your life shows you the love of God?*
3. *What can you do to share the love of God with others?*

It would also be appropriate to elaborate on the charity you will be supporting this year. You can share your own feelings about the charity, or you can read a letter from someone who works with the charity. Invite someone in to speak about the need and how the students can participate in helping.

Song

"Holy Is Your Name" (Canticle of Mary), CD/CS–#4, mb–#4

RITUAL ACTION

Ritually bring forth items for this year's mission. Have a special box or container to put these items in each time. If you have time, you can also pray with each student, inviting them to come forward, saying, "I invite each of you to come forward and to place your hand on the Scripture as I place my hand on top of yours. Together we will pray that the word of God will inspire you this year." When you are with each student, say, "N., may the words of Scripture inspire your actions this year. May the Father, and the Son, and the Holy Spirit be with you. Amen!"

INTERCESSIONS

"General Intercessions," in music collection or:

Leader: Let us come before God with our needs.

Reader: For our Church and all who lead us in our journey of faith. Let us pray to the Lord.

All: **Lord, hear our prayer.**

Reader: For our world and all who work for the dignity of all humanity. Let us pray to the Lord.

For all those in need, especially. . . *(name the charity)*. Let us pray to the Lord.

Insert your own intentions here.

For those who are ill. Let us pray to the Lord.

For those who have died. Let us pray to the Lord.

LORD'S PRAYER

Leader: Let us join in the words that Christ has given us.

All: **Our Father . . . for the kingdom, the power, and the glory are yours, now and for ever. Amen.**

CONCLUDING RITE

"Final Blessing," CD/CS–#19, mb–#25, or:

Leader: The Lord be with you.
All: **And also with you.**
Leader: May almighty God bless us, the Father, the Son, ✠ and the Holy Spirit.
All: **Amen!**
Leader: Our celebration has ended. Let us go forth to love and serve our God.
All: **Thanks be to God.**

Concluding Song
"Prayer for Peace," CD/CS–#13, mb–#16

The Journey and the Promise

UNIT 2
CHAPTERS 5–8

Getting Started

In this liturgy the leader is to pray with each of the students individually. This ritual action should be done in silence. Work on developing a style of prayer that would be beneficial to this ritual. Remember to focus on the students' need to serve the greater world. There are many ways the students can be of service. You can focus on these or on the charity the group is supporting this year.

INTRODUCTORY RITES

Opening Song

"Blest Are You, O God" (Canticle of Zachary), CD/CS–#7, mb–#7

Leader: In the name of the Father, and of the Son, and of the Holy Spirit.
All: **Amen!**
Leader: The Lord be with you.
All: **And also with you.**

Opening Comments

Leader: As we continue on our journey this year, we remember God's promise to always be with us. This is evident in the lives of the saints—the people of faith—who have preceded us. Let us remember the special ways they served the people of God.

Opening Prayer

Leader: Let us pray. *(orans gesture)*
Lord, receive all our liberties, our memories, and our understanding.
All that we are and all that we possess comes from you, O God.
May we surrender all our lives to your love and grace.
May our service to others always praise you as the God who lives and reigns for ever and ever. Amen.

SCRIPTURE READING

Isaiah 42:1–4

A Bible should be on the prayer table. Reverence the Bible and then lift and read directly from it.

Leader: A reading from the Book of Isaiah.

Here is my servant! I have made him strong. He is my chosen one; I am pleased with him. I have given him my Spirit, and he will bring justice to the nations. He won't shout or yell or call out in the streets. He won't break off a bent reed or put out a dying flame, but he will make sure that justice is done. He won't quit or give up until he brings justice everywhere on earth, and people in foreign nations long for his teaching.

Leader: The word of the Lord.
All: **Thanks be to God.**

Reflection

Share with the group your feelings about the Scripture reading. Use these questions for your personal reflection.

1. *Which saints have inspired your faith life?*
2. *What does it mean for you to be a servant of the Lord?*
3. *Where in the world do you see a need for justice? How can the Church help foster this?*

Song

"God's People" (Psalm 100), CD/CS–#2, mb–#2

RITUAL ACTION

Leader: The saints' lives are an inspiration to us as we do the work of the Lord. The saints spent much time in prayer. Let us spend time praying with one another, asking God to be with us. We ask God in silence to allow his Spirit to be with us. As I place my hands on yours, let us concentrate on the words of Scripture: "Here is my servant! I have made him strong. He is my chosen one; I am pleased with him. I have given him my Spirit."

*Each student comes forward and the catechist prays with each one individually. Place your hands on the student's and then **silently** pray. At the end of the silent prayer, invite the students to come forward with their gift for the charity they are supporting.*

INTERCESSIONS

"General Intercessions," in music collection or:

Leader: Let us come before God with our needs.

Reader: For the Church and all who lead us in faith. Let us pray to the Lord.
All: **Lord, hear our prayer.**

Reader: For those who are in need of our help, especially. . . *(name the charity)*. Let us pray to the Lord.

Insert your own intentions here.

For those who are ill. Let us pray to the Lord.

For those who have died. Let us pray to the Lord.

LORD'S PRAYER

Leader: Let us join in the words that Christ has given us.

All: **Our Father . . . for the kingdom, the power, and the glory are yours, now and for ever. Amen.**

CONCLUDING RITE   "Final Blessing," CD/CS–#19, mb–#25, or:

Leader: The Lord be with you.
All: **And also with you.**
Leader: May almighty God bless us, the Father, the Son, ✠ and the Holy Spirit.
All: **Amen!**
Leader: Our celebration has ended. Let us go forth to love and serve our God.
All: **Thanks be to God.**

Concluding Song
"Walking by Faith," CD/CS–#1, mb–#1

The One Who Is to Come

UNIT 3
CHAPTERS 9–12

Getting Started

If possible, celebrate this service during the Season of Advent. Gather around your Advent wreath or the parish's Advent wreath. This service will support the school- or parish-wide celebration for Advent and may be celebrated before or after that service.

INTRODUCTORY RITES

Opening Song

"Advent Gathering: Make Ready the Way/Come, O Lord," CD/CS–#3, mb–#3
Use the Blessing of the Advent Wreath and "Come, O Lord" as you light the appropriate number of candles.

Leader: In the name of the Father, and of the Son, and of the Holy Spirit.
All: **Amen!**
Leader: The Lord be with you.
All: **And also with you.**

Opening Comments

Leader: As we gather in this Season of Advent, let us remember our call to serve others and to always do this in prayer.

Opening Prayer

Leader: Let us pray. *(orans gesture)*
God of light,
your promise of love is evident in the gift of your Son in our life.
May we always reflect on Christ as the source
of our actions and service.
May the light of Christ always illuminate our journey of faith.
We ask this through Christ our Lord. Amen!

SCRIPTURE READING

Ecclesiastes 3:1–8

A Bible should be on the prayer table. Reverence the Bible and then lift and read directly from it.

Leader: A reading from the Book of Ecclesiastes.

Everything on earth has its own time and its own season. There is a time for birth and death, planting and reaping, for killing and healing, destroying and building, for crying and laughing, weeping and dancing, for throwing stones and gathering stones, embracing and parting. There is a time for finding and losing, keeping and giving, for tearing and sewing, listening and speaking. There is also a time for love and hate, for war and peace.

Leader: The word of the Lord.
All: **Thanks be to God.**

Reflection

Share with the group your feelings about the Scripture reading. Use these questions for your personal reflection.

1. *How is the gospel message of "a time and season for everything" reflected in your own life?*
2. *Can you define moments when the love of God was present in your life?*
3. *How can moments of peace be fostered and celebrated during the Advent Season?*

Song

"To You, O Lord" (Psalm 25), CD/CS–#6, mb–#6

RITUAL ACTION

Continue the collection for your charity. Focus on the Season of Advent as being a preparation for Christmas. If you have not been able to do a continuous contribution to a charity, this may be a good time to do a one-time collection. Think about adopting a family and having the group buy gifts for them.

INTERCESSIONS

"General Intercessions," in music collection or:

Leader: Let us come before God with our needs.

Reader: For the Church and all who help to bring Christ to others. Let us pray to the Lord.

All: **Lord, hear our prayer.**

Reader: For those who lead our world and strive to be lights of peace. Let us pray to the Lord.

For those who seek the light of Christ in their darkened world. Let us pray to the Lord.

Insert your own intentions here.

For those who are ill. Let us pray to the Lord.

For those who have died. Let us pray to the Lord.

LORD'S PRAYER

Leader: Let us join in the words that Christ has given us.

All: **Our Father . . . for the kingdom, the power, and the glory are yours, now and for ever. Amen.**

CONCLUDING RITE   "Final Blessing," CD/CS–#19, mb–#25, or:

Leader: The Lord be with you.

All: **And also with you**.

Leader: May almighty God bless us, the Father, the Son, ✠ and the Holy Spirit.

All: **Amen!**

Leader: Our celebration has ended. Let us go forth to love and serve our God.

All: **Thanks be to God.**

Concluding Song
"Prayer for Peace," CD/CS–#13, mb–#16

Founded on the Gospels

UNIT 4
CHAPTERS 13–16

Getting Started

During this Christmas Season we need to focus on the rebirth of Jesus in our life. In this service we will renew our own baptismal promises.

INTRODUCTORY RITES

Opening Song

"Blest Are You, O God" (Canticle of Zachary), CD/CS–#7, mb–#7

Leader: In the name of the Father, and of the Son, and of the Holy Spirit.
All: **Amen!**
Leader: The Lord be with you.
All: **And also with you.**

Opening Comments

Leader: During this Season of Christmas let us reflect on Jesus' love for all of us. He loves us so much that he came to live with us. Let us remember how Jesus served all people.

Opening Prayer

Leader: Let us pray. *(orans gesture)*
Loving God and Father,
your love is present in Christ your Son.
May we always follow Jesus' example to be of service to those in need.
May we be inspired to do works of charity in this new year.
We ask this through Christ our Lord. Amen!

SCRIPTURE READING

Luke 4:16–21

A Bible should be on the prayer table. Reverence the Bible and then lift and read directly from it.

Leader: The Lord be with you.
All: **And also with you.**
Leader: A reading from the holy Gospel according to Luke.
All: **Glory to you, O Lord.**

Jesus went back to Nazareth, where he had been brought up, and as usual he went to the meeting place on the Sabbath. When he stood up to read from the Scriptures, he was given the book of Isaiah the prophet. He opened it and read, "The Lord's Spirit has come to me, because he has chosen me to tell the good news to the poor. The Lord has sent me to announce freedom for prisoners, to give sight to the blind, to free everyone who suffers, and to say, 'This is the year the Lord has chosen.'" Jesus closed the book, then handed it back to the man in charge and sat down. Everyone in the meeting place looked straight at Jesus. Then Jesus said to them, "What you have just heard me read has come true today."

Leader: The gospel of the Lord.
All: **Praise to you, Lord Jesus Christ.**

Reflection
Share with the group your feelings about the Scripture reading. Use these questions for your personal reflection.
1. *When have you witnessed someone working for the good of others?*
2. *Who moves you to serve the needs of this world?*
3. *What new thing can you do this year that would serve the needs of people who are poor?*

Song
"Like the Sweet Fragrance" (Canticle of Sirach), CD/CS–#11, mb–#13

RITUAL ACTION

Renewal of Baptismal Promises
If possible, gather around the parish font or use holy water from the parish. If not, gather in a circle and finish the ritual by having the students sign one another with the Sign of the Cross.

Leader: Do you reject evil and renew your commitment to Jesus Christ?
All: **I do.**

Leader: Do you believe in God, the Father almighty, creator of heaven and earth?
All: **I do.**

Leader: Do you believe in Jesus Christ, Son of God?
All: **I do.**

Leader: Do you believe in the Holy Spirit?
All: **I do.**

Leader: Will you proclaim by word and example the good news of God in Christ?
All: **I will, with God's help.**

Leader: Will you strive for justice and peace among all people?
All: **I will, with God's help.**

Leader: *(if water is present)* Let us come to the holy water and sign one another.

Have the students bring up their gifts for charity.

LORD'S PRAYER

Leader: Let us join in the words that Christ has given us.

All: **Our Father . . . for the kingdom, the power, and the glory are yours, now and for ever. Amen.**

CONCLUDING RITE

"Final Blessing," CD/CS–#19, mb–#25, or:

Leader: The Lord be with you.

All: **And also with you**.

Leader: May almighty God bless us, the Father, the Son, ✠ and the Holy Spirit.

All: **Amen!**

Leader: Our celebration has ended. Let us go forth to love and serve our God.

All: **Thanks be to God.**

Concluding Song
"Walking by Faith," CD/CS–#1, mb–#1

True to the Promise

UNIT 5
CHAPTERS 17–20

Getting Started

Celebrate this prayer service during the Lenten Season. Connect the reading, which many are familiar, with the acts of service that your group may be doing.

INTRODUCTORY RITES

Opening Song
"Jesus, Heal Us," CD/CS–#16, mb–#20

Leader: In the name of the Father, and of the Son, and of the Holy Spirit.
All: **Amen!**
Leader: The Lord be with you.
All: **And also with you.**

Opening Comments

Leader: In this Season of Lent, we are called to perform acts of love and justice, and to serve those in our world who are in need. Our lives must be filled with the courage to love as Christ loved—unconditionally.

Opening Prayer

Leader: Let us pray. *(orans gesture)*
God of love and justice,
your words show us how your love will never fail.
During this season of fasting, prayers, and almsgiving—this Season of Lent—may we always show love for all humanity.
We ask this through Christ our Lord. Amen!

SCRIPTURE READING

1 Corinthians 13:4–8a

A Bible should be on the prayer table. Reverence the Bible and then lift and read directly from it.

Leader: A reading from the First Letter of Paul to the Corinthians.

Love is kind and patient, never jealous, boastful, proud or rude. Love isn't selfish or quick tempered. It doesn't keep a record of wrongs that others do. Love rejoices in the truth, but not in evil. Love is always supportive, loyal, hopeful, and trusting. Love never fails!

Leader: The word of the Lord.
All: **Thanks be to God.**

Reflection

Share with the group your feelings about the Scripture reading. Use these questions for your personal reflection.
1. *Which description of love moves your spirit the most?*
2. *How are these descriptions of love different from what the world teaches us about so-called "love"?*

3. *What inhibits you from always acting out of love toward other people? How do you overcome the obstacle(s)?*

Song
"Lord, Be with Me" (Psalm 91), CD/CS–#14, mb–#17

RITUAL ACTION   *During the prayer, which is found on p. 149 of the student textbook, light some candles of different sizes. After the prayer, invite the students to come forward with their gifts for the class charity.*

Leader: Let us call upon the Spirit to be with us as we pray for all of humanity. *Light candles.*

All: **Come, Holy Spirit,**
fill the hearts of your faithful,
and kindle in them the fire of your love.
Send forth your Spirit and we will be created.
And you will renew the face of the earth.
Lord, by the light of the Holy Spirit
you have taught the hearts of your faithful.
In the same Spirit help us choose what is right
and always rejoice in your consolation.
We ask this through Christ our Lord. Amen.

Leader: Let us now bring forward our gifts for our charity.

LORD'S PRAYER
Leader: Let us join in the words that Christ has given us.

All: **Our Father . . . for the kingdom, the power, and the glory are yours,**
now and for ever. Amen.

CONCLUDING RITE   "Final Blessing," CD/CS–#19, mb–#25, or:

Leader: The Lord be with you.
All: **And also with you.**
Leader: May almighty God bless us, the Father, the Son, ✠ and the Holy Spirit.
All: **Amen!**
Leader: Our celebration has ended. Let us go forth to love and serve our God.
All: **Thanks be to God.**

Concluding Song
"Blest Are They," CD/CS–#17, mb–#22

Sacraments of Salvation

Getting Started

During this prayer service we will contemplate on Holy Week. Seriously reflect on the words of mission expressed during Holy Thursday. You may want to include your group's donation to charity with the offertory during the service on Holy Thursday. Discuss this with the coordinator of the Holy Thursday liturgy. Another option would be to attend the diocesan Mass of the Oils instead of celebrating this liturgy. This special Mass is celebrated during Holy Week and is often a time when members of the clergy renew their commitment to ministry. This would support the study of commitment and promise in this unit.

INTRODUCTORY RITES

Opening Song

"The Bread That Gives Life," CD/CS–#9, mb–#10

Leader:	In the name of the Father, and of the Son, and of the Holy Spirit.
All:	**Amen!**
Leader:	The Lord be with you.
All:	**And also with you.**

Opening Comments

Leader: As we approach the special liturgies of Holy Week, we reflect on how Jesus calls each of us to serve all people.

Opening Prayer

Leader: Let us pray. *(orans gesture)*
Loving God,
you speak to us and nourish us through the life of this community.
In the name of Jesus,
we ask you to send your Spirit to us
so that men and women, young and old,
will respond to your call to service and leadership in the Church.
We ask this through Christ our Lord. Amen!

SCRIPTURE READING

John 13:1–15

A Bible should be on the prayer table. Reverence the Bible and then lift and read directly from it.

Leader:	The Lord be with you.
All:	**And also with you.**
Leader:	A reading from the holy Gospel according to John.
All:	**Glory to you, O Lord.**

It was before Passover, and Jesus knew that the time had come for him to leave this world and to return to the Father. He had always loved his followers in this world, and he loved them to the very end. Even before the evening meal started, the devil had made Judas, the son of Simon Iscariot, decide to betray Jesus. Jesus knew that he had come from God and would

go back to God. He also knew that the Father had given him complete power. So during the meal Jesus got up, removed his outer garment, and wrapped a towel around his waist. He put some water into a large bowl. Then he began washing his disciples' feet and drying them with the towel he was wearing.

But when he came to Simon Peter, that disciple asked, "Lord, are you going to wash my feet?" Jesus answered, "You don't really know what I am doing, but later you will understand." "You will never wash my feet!" Peter replied. "If I don't wash you," Jesus told him, "you don't really belong to me." Peter said, "Lord, don't wash just my feet. Wash my hands and my head." Jesus answered, "People who have bathed and are clean all over need to wash just their feet. And you, my disciples, are clean, except for one of you." Jesus knew who would betray him. That is why he said, "except for one of you."

After Jesus had washed his disciple's feet and had put his outer garment back on, he sat down again. Then he said: "Do you understand what I have done? You call me your teacher and Lord, and you should, because that is who I am. And if your Lord and teacher has washed your feet, you should do the same for each other. I have set the example, and you should do for each other exactly what I have done for you."

Leader: The gospel of the Lord.
All: **Praise to you, Lord Jesus Christ.**

Reflection
Share with the group your feelings about the Scripture reading. Use these questions for your personal reflection.
1. *What would it have been like to have your own feet washed by Jesus?*
2. *What does it mean for you to wash feet? Why would you wash someone's feet?*
3. *Whose feet are you asked to wash?*
4. *Who has washed feet in this world? Reflect on the life of Mother Teresa.*

Song
"Raining Down Manna" (Psalm 78), CD/CS–#15, mb–#19

RITUAL ACTION *Invite the students to come forward with their contribution to the charity of choice. Also consider doing a foot washing ceremony similar to how the parish celebrates this rite during Holy Thursday.*

INTERCESSIONS "General Intercessions," in music collection or:

Leader: Let us come before God with our needs.

Reader: For the Church and all who are called to serve the people of God. Let us pray to the Lord.
All: **Lord, hear our prayer.**

Reader: For those who lead countries in ways of peace. Let us pray to the Lord.

For those who feel left out and neglected. Let us pray to the Lord.

Insert your own intentions here.

For those who are ill. Let us pray to the Lord.

For those who have died. Let us pray to the Lord.

LORD'S PRAYER
Leader: Let us join in the words that Christ has given us.

All: **Our Father . . . for the kingdom, the power, and the glory are yours, now and for ever. Amen.**

CONCLUDING RITE
"Final Blessing," CD/CS–#19, mb–#25, or:

Leader: The Lord be with you.
All: **And also with you.**
Leader: May almighty God bless us, the Father, the Son, ✠ and the Holy Spirit.
All: **Amen!**
Leader: Our celebration has ended. Let us go forth to love and serve our God.
All: **Thanks be to God.**

Concluding Song
"Song of the Body of Christ," CD/CS–#18, mb–#24

Journey to the Future

UNIT 7
CHAPTERS 25–28

Getting Started

As this is the last service of the year, plan to celebrate around the parish baptismal font. You may want to invite a representative from the charity you have been working with and have them receive the class gift for the last time. Remember to send the students forth with a strong message of mission.

INTRODUCTORY
RITES

Opening Song

Verses 1 and 2 from "People of God/Alleluia," CD/CS–#8, mb–#8

Leader: In the name of the Father, and of the Son, and of the Holy Spirit.
All: **Amen!**
Leader: The Lord be with you.
All: **And also with you.**

Opening Comments

Leader: As we come to an end of another year of religious education, let us turn toward God and celebrate our call to mission.

Opening Prayer

Leader: Let us pray. *(orans gesture)*
Almighty and eternal God,
you gather the scattered sheep
and watch over those you have gathered.
Look kindly on all who follow Jesus, your Son.
You have marked them with the seal of one baptism;
now make them one in the fullness of faith
and unite them in the bond of love.
We ask this through Christ our Lord. Amen!

SCRIPTURE
READING

Galatians 3:26–28

A Bible should be on the prayer table. Reverence the Bible and then lift and read directly from it.

Leader: A reading from the Letter of Paul to the Galatians.

All of you are God's children because of your faith in Christ Jesus. And when you were baptized, it was as though you had put on Christ in the same way you put on new clothes. Faith in Christ Jesus is what makes each of you equal with each other, whether you are a Jew or a Greek, a slave or a free person, a man or a woman.

Leader: The word of the Lord.
All: **Thanks be to God.**

Reflection

Share with the group your feelings about the Scripture reading. Use these questions for your personal reflection.

1. *How do you interpret the image of faith as expressed in this reading?*
2. *What has happened this year, catechetically, that has touched you personally?*
3. *What are the challenges that you will take with you on your journey of faith?*

Song

"This Is the Day" (Psalm 118), CD/CS–#12, mb–#14

RITUAL ACTION   *Use the "Greeting and Thanksgiving Over Water Already Blessed" found in "People of God/Alleluia," CD/CS–#8, mb–#8. At the end of the rite, have the students come forward for a final contribution to their charity.*

INTERCESSIONS   "General Intercessions," in music collection or:

Leader: Let us come before God with our needs.

Reader: For the Church and all who walk by faith.
            Let us pray to the Lord.

All: **Lord, hear our prayer.**

Reader: For leaders of this world and all countries trying to
            serve the needs of humanity.
            Let us pray to the Lord.

            For those who are neglected because of
            the world's insensitivity to their needs.
            Let us pray to the Lord.

            Insert your own intentions here.

            For those who are ill.
            Let us pray to the Lord.

            For those who have died.
            Let us pray to the Lord.

LORD'S PRAYER
Leader: Let us join in the words that Christ has given us.

All: **Our Father . . . for the kingdom, the power, and the glory are yours,
        now and for ever. Amen.**

CONCLUDING RITE   "Final Blessing," CD/CS–#19, mb–#25, or:

Leader: The Lord be with you.
All: **And also with you.**
Leader: May almighty God bless us, the Father, the Son, ✠ and the Holy Spirit.
All: **Amen!**
Leader: Our celebration has ended. Let us go forth to love and serve our God.
All: **Thanks be to God.**

Concluding Song
"Walking by Faith," CD/CS–#1, mb–#1

OTHER MUSICAL SUGGESTIONS

The following are other musical suggestions that may be incorporated with the *Walking by Faith* Music and Liturgy Resource editions. These seven categories are not meant to suggest that these songs are for only one specific grade. It is suggested that you look through these songs and decide for yourself where they might fit best. You can also check your parish's musical resources for other specific liturgical needs, such as Advent, Christmas, Lent, and Easter. Also included is the item number of where it appears in GIA's hymnal, *Gather Comprehensive*. Where applicable, the GIA order numbers are included.

CREATION

All Creatures of Our God and King–LASST UNS ERFREUEN, (GC533)
All You Works of God–Haugen, G-3481, (GC492)
For the Beauty of the Earth–DIX, (GC572)
Joyful, Joyful, We Adore You–HYMN TO JOY, (GC528)
Morning Has Broken–BUNESSAN, (GC756)
Sing Out, Earth and Skies–Haugen, G-3590, (GC499)
You Are the Voice–Haas, G-2705, (GC549)

GOD

Creator of the Stars of Night–CONDITOR ALME SIDERUM, (GC337)
Joyful, Joyful, We Adore You–HYMN TO JOY, (GC528)
God of Day and God of Darkness–BEACH SPRING, G-3595, (GC761)
There Is One Lord–from *Music from Taizé*, G-2778, (GC809)
There's a Wideness in God's Mercy–IN BABILONE, (GC626)
We Are God's Work of Art–Haugen, G-3189, (GC808)
Without Seeing You–Haas, G-3928, (GC844)

JESUS CHRIST

All Hail the Power of Jesus' Name–CORONATION or DIADEMATA, (GC484)
I Heard the Voice of Jesus Say–KINGSFOLD, (GC646)
I Know That My Redeemer Lives–DUKE STREET, (GC430)
In the Lord I'll Be Ever Thankful–from *Songs & Prayers from Taizé*, G-3719, (GC566)
Now We Remain–Haas, G-2709, (GC694)
Send Us Your Spirit–Haas, G-3340, (GC470)
What Wondrous Love Is This–WONDROUS LOVE, (GC627)

THE CHURCH

All Are Welcome–Haugen, G-4274, (GC753)
Bring Forth the Kingdom–Haugen, G-3592, (GC658)
Christ Is Made the Sure Foundation–ST. THOMAS, (GC662)
Faith of Our Fathers–ST. CATHERINE, (GC600)
Table Song–Haas, G-3694, (GC849)
The Church's One Foundation–AURELIA, (GC661)
We Gather Together–KREMSER, (GC571)

CHRISTIAN MORALITY

Amazing Grace–NEW BRITAIN, (GC612)
Lord, Whose Love in Humble Service–HOLY MANNA or IN BABILONE, (GC681)
Make Me a Channel of Your Peace–Temple, (GC–726)
May Love Be Ours, (Not for Tongues)–Joncas, G-3158, (GC623)
Servant Song–Fisher, G-3730, (GC683)
The Harvest of Justice–Haas, G-3582, (GC711)
Where Charity and Love Prevail–CHRISTIAN LOVE, (GC625)

THE SACRAMENTS

At That First Eucharist–UNDE ET MEMORES, (GC852)
Come Down, O Love Divine–DOWN AMPNEY, (GC465)
Jesus, Wine of Peace–Haas, G-3027, (GC817)
O Holy Spirit, by Whose Breath–VENI CREATOR SPIRITUS or LASST UNS ERFREUEN,, (GC461)
Send Us Your Spirit–Haas, G-3340, (GC470)
Spirit-Friend–Colvin, G-4598, (GC467)
There Is One Lord–from *Music from Taizé*, G-2778, (GC809)

SALVATION HISTORY

At the Lamb's High Feast We Sing–SALZBURG, (GC433)
I Am the Bread of Life–Toolan, G-1693, (GC828)
O God, Our Help in Ages Past–ST. ANNE, (GC614)
Onward to the Kingdom–MARIE'S WEDDING, Haas, G-3954, (GC660)
Take and Eat–Joncas, G-3435, (GC831)
The Kingdom of God–LAUDATE DOMINUM, (GC655)
There's a Wideness in God's Mercy–IN BABILONE, (GC626)

Special Thanks

There are many people to thank when writing a book like this. It is through their wisdom and confidence that allows the spirit of prayer to flow onto these pages. I am sure I am forgetting someone, but know that all those who have mentored me and shared their prayer life with me has made this book come into being.

Thank you to David Haas for the collaborative inspiration of the music and for allowing me into the studio to watch his creative process take life. Thanks to Alec and Ed Harris, Bob Batastini, and Michael Cymbala from GIA for their willingness to enter the world of catechesis. To Matt Thibeau and Marge Elgin-Krawzuck and all the folks at BROWN-ROA who believed in the integration of liturgy and catechesis. Also, thank you to the staff of the American Bible Society for their assistance in helping me use the *Contemporary English Version* in these liturgies. Everyone there has truly made the word of God come alive!

Personal thanks to Rev. Bob Stoeckig who helped me realize the blank screen on my computer could actually have words. My special friends in Minneapolis–Jean Bross, Jeff Judge, David Fischer, Patty Stromen, Kate Cuddy, and the Nicpons who nursed me back to health in both mind and spirit when I didn't think this would ever get done. Thanks to Steve, Judy, and Alicia Petrunak for giving me space to be honest, and making me honest in my writing. Thanks to Joe and Pat Hudetz and their daughter Sarah who sat through hours of my reading of prayers and texts.

Thank you to my mentor, Sister Mary Gleason, IBVM for her willingness to let me see the Christ that has inspired her in her catechetical world. Thanks to my sister, Deborah Shimek, who is "super-teacher" and who always challenged me to think of the teacher who has to pray these prayers, and to my parents, Robert and Rosemarie, who were my teachers of liturgy.

Finally, a very special thank you to Marilyn Bowers Gorun from BROWN-ROA and Jeff Mickus from GIA Publications, editors of this portion of the project. Their tenacity, care for catechesis and the child, and overall understanding of how I work has made this all seem worthwhile. Editors go unthanked way too often. Thank you, thank you, thank you!

To everyone, you are special as we all walk by faith!

Robert W. Piercy Jr.
November 1997

DAVID HAAS

David Haas lives in St. Paul, Minnesota, and is the director of The Emmaus Center for Music, Prayer and Ministry. A former parish music and liturgy director, he is active as a cantor, pianist, guitarist, author, choir director, concert performer, teacher, workshop leader, recording artist, and composer of music for worship. Highly regarded as one of the preeminent liturgical composers in the English-speaking world, David has produced over twenty collections and recordings of liturgical music, including *Who Calls You by Name,* Vol. 1 and 2 (GIA), an ongoing series of music for Christian Initiation. For the recording of *I Shall See God* (GIA), David was nominated for a Grammy Award in 1991. His most recent collections of music include *Where the River Flows, Psalms for the Church Year, Volume 8,* and *Throughout All Time* (GIA). His latest live recording, *Glory Day,* is not only a full-length feature video, but, double compact disc as well (published with GIA and St. Anthony Messenger Press). Together with Bonnie Faber, he has produced the video series *With Every Note I Sing: The Ministry of the Cantor* (GIA). David's music has appeared in many hymnals and anthologies, and he was one of the consultants for the revised edition of Gather (GIA).

David has traveled throughout the United States, Canada, Europe, Australia, and Israel as a keynote speaker, workshop presenter, retreat leader and concert performer, and is quite active in the work of the Order of Christian Initiation of Adults, being a team member for the North American Forum on the Catechumenate. David has collaborated with Thomas Morris on a cassette series of talks on Initiation entitled *Christian Initiation: Liturgical, Catechetical and Musical Dimensions* (St. Anthony Messenger Press). As an author, David's articles have appeared in Pastoral Music, Modern Liturgy, Catechumenate, The GIA Quarterly, and he was one of the contributing authors for A *Catechumenate Needs Everybody* (Liturgy Training Publications). An author of several books, David is well known for his many books of prayers, especially *Psalm Prayers* (St. Anthony Messenger Press) and *With Every Note I Sing* (GIA). His latest books include a two-volume series of prayers for the liturgical year entitled *Praying with the Word* (St. Anthony Messenger Press) and *Dear God...Prayers for Children* (Crossroad Publications).

ROBERT W. PIERCY

Robert Piercy is president of R.W.P. Consulting Services, a consulting firm for publishers and dioceses across the United States. He is well known for his work in rites and rituals with children. Presently, Piercy serves as national catechetical director for GIA Publications, senior Catholic consultant for the American Bible Society and publishing consultant for Living the Good News. He co-authored A *Guide to the Lectionary for Masses with Children* and was project coordinator for A *Common Sense for Parish Life and Infant Baptism: Catechesis and Mystagogy*—all from Liturgy Training Publications of Chicago. He has served as a parish liturgy director in the Joliet and Chicago dioceses. His work nationally has taken him across the United States as a speaker for many major conferences. He has also served as liturgy director for the Great Lakes Pastoral Gathering and annually serves as liturgy director for the National Parish Catechetical Directors convocation of the National Catholic Educators of America convention. Robert has worked in the area of visual arts of music sung in churches. He served as artistic director and choreographer for the video *Glory Day...David Haas and Friends in Concert,* published by GIA Publications and St. Anthony Messenger Press.

Other Resources for Children from GIA Publications, Inc.

When Children Gather
by Robert W. Piercy and Vivian E. Williams

G-4757	20 Eucharistic Liturgies for the School Year
G-4807	20 Prayer Services for the Liturgical Year
G-4806FS	Full Score
G-4806P	Student Melody Book
CD-402	Double Compact Disc
CS-402	Double Cassette Set

How Excellent • Songs for Teens, Volumes I & II

Volume I
CD-377	Compact Disc
CS-377	Cassette
G-4628	Music Collection (includes Songbook)
G-4628A	Songbook for both volumes (melody/words)

Volume II
CD-378	Compact Disc
CS-378	Cassette
G-4629	Music Collection (includes Songbook)

We Are God's People: Psalms for the Family of God
by Jeanne Cotter

CD-344	Compact Disc
CS-344	Cassette
G-4293	Music Collection
G-4293P	Performance Edition